AA GLOVEBOX ATLAS
SCOTLAND
SCOTLAND'S CLEAREST MAPPING

Atlas co

Scale 1:250,000 or 3.9

C000135609

Route planner	II–III
Map pages	IV
Atlas Symbols	1
Road maps 1:250,000 scale	2–83
Western Isles 1:700,000 scale	84–85
Orkney Islands 1:636,000 scale	86
Shetland Islands 1:636,000 scale	87
Mileage chart	88
Index to place names	89–108
County, administrative area map	89
Place name index	90–108

1st edition August 2008

© Automobile Association
Developments Limited 2008

Cartography:
All cartography in this atlas edited,
designed and produced by the
Mapping Services Department of
AA Publishing (A03840).

 **Enabled by** **Ordnance Survey** This product includes
mapping data licensed from Ordnance
Survey® with the permission of the
Controller of Her Majesty's Stationery
Office. © Crown copyright 2008.
All rights reserved.
Licence number 100021153.

Publisher's notes:
Published by AA Publishing (a trading
name of Automobile Association
Developments Limited, whose
registered office is Fanum House,
Basing View, Basingstoke, Hampshire
RG21 4EA, UK. Registered number
1878835).

ISBN: 978 0 7495 5925 0

A CIP catalogue record for this book is
available from The British Library.

Disclaimer:
The contents of this atlas are
believed to be correct at the time of
the latest revision, it will not contain
any subsequent amended, new
or temporary information including
diversions and traffic control or
enforcement systems. The publishers
cannot be held responsible or liable for
any loss or damage occasioned to any
person acting or refraining from action
as a result of any use or reliance on
material in this atlas, nor for any errors,
omissions or changes in such material.
This does not affect your statutory
rights.

The publishers would welcome
information to correct any errors or
omissions and to keep this atlas up
to date. Please write to the Atlas
Editor, AA Publishing, The Automobile
Association, Fanum House,
Basing View, Basingstoke, Hampshire
RG21 4EA, UK.
E-mail: roadatlasfeedback@theaa.com

Acknowledgements:
AA Publishing would like to thank
the following for their assistance in
producing this atlas:

RoadPilot® Information on
fixed speed
camera locations provided by RoadPilot
© 2008 RoadPilot® Driving Technology.
Information on truckstops and
transport cafés kindly provided by
John Eden (www.transportcafe.co.uk).
Forestry Commission, Historic
Scotland, National Trust for Scotland,
RSPB, Scottish Natural Heritage.

Printer:
Printed in China by Leo Paper Group.
Paper: 100gsm Matt Coated.

Route planner

Scottish island ferries

Hebridean island and west coast ferries
www.calmac.co.uk   *01475 650100*

Ferries to Orkney and Shetland
www.northlinkferries.co.uk   *0845 6000 449*
www.pentlandferries.co.uk   *01856 831226*

Orkney and Shetland inter-island ferries
www.orkneyferries.co.uk   *01856 872044*
www.shetland.gov.uk/ferries   *01595 743970*

Restricted junctions

M8 Edinburgh - Bishopton

Junction	Westbound	Eastbound
8	No access from M73 (southbound) or from A8 (eastbound) & A89	No exit to M73 (northbound) or to A8 (westbound) & A89
9	Access only	Exit only
13	Access only from M80 (southbound)	Exit only to M80 (northbound)
14	Access only	Exit only
16	Exit only to A804	Access only from A879
17	Exit only to A82	No restriction
18	Access only from A82 (eastbound)	Exit only to A814
19	No access from A814 (westbound)	Exit only to A814 (westbound)
20	Exit only	Access only
21	Access only	Exit only to A8
22	Exit only to M77 (southbound)	Access only from M77 (northbound)
23	Exit only to B768	Access only from B768
25	No access or exit from or to A8	No access or exit from or to A8
25A	Exit only	Access only
28	Exit only	Access only
28A	Exit only to A737	Access only from A737

M9 Edinburgh - Dunblane

Junction	Northwestbound	Southeastbound
1A	Access only to A90	Access only from A90
2	Access only	Exit only
3	Exit only	Access only
6	Access only from A904	Exit only to A905
8	Exit only to M876 (southwestbound)	Access only from M876 (northeastbound)

M73 East of Glasgow

Junction	Northbound	Southbound
2	No access from or exit to A89. No access from M8 (eastbound).	No access from or exit to A89. No exit to M8 (westbound)
3	Exit only to A80 (northeastbound)	Access only from A80 (southwestbound)

M74 and A74(M) Glasgow - Gretna

Junction	Southbound	Northbound
2	Access only from A763	Exit only to A763
3	Exit only	Access only
7	Exit only to A72	Access only from A72
9	Exit only to B7078	No access or exit
10	Access only from B7078	No restrictions
11	Exit only to B7078	Access only from B7078
12	Access only from A70	Exit only to A70
18	Access only from B723	Exit only to B723
21	Exit only to B6357	Access only from B6357
with B7076	Access only	Exit only
Gretna Green	Exit only	Access only
with A75	Access only from A75	Exit only to A75
with A6071	Exit only to A74 (southbound)	Access only from A74 (northbound)

M77 South of Glasgow

Junction	Southbound	Northbound
with M8 (jct 22)	No access from M8 (eastbound)	No exit to M8 (westbound)
4	Exit only	Access only
6	Exit only	Access only)

M80 Stepps Bypass

Junction	Northeastbound	Southwestbound
1	Access only	No restriction
3	Exit only	Access only

M80 Bonnybridge - Stirling

Junction	Northbound	Southbound
5	Exit only to M876 (northeastbound)	Access only from M876 (southwestbound)

M90 Forth Road Bridge - Perth

Junction	Northbound	Southbound
2A	Exit only to A92 (eastbound)	Access only from A92 (westbound)
7	Access only from A91	Exit only to A91
8	Exit only to A91	Access only from A91
10	No access from A912. No exit to A912 (southbound)	No access from A912 (northbound). No exit to A912

M876 Bonnybridge - Kincardine Bridge

Junction	Northeastbound	Southwestbound
with M80 (jct 5)	Access only from M80 (northbound)	Exit only to M80 (southbound)
2	Exit only to A9	Access only from A9
with M9 (jct 8)	Exit only to M9 (eastbound)	Access only from M9 (westbound)

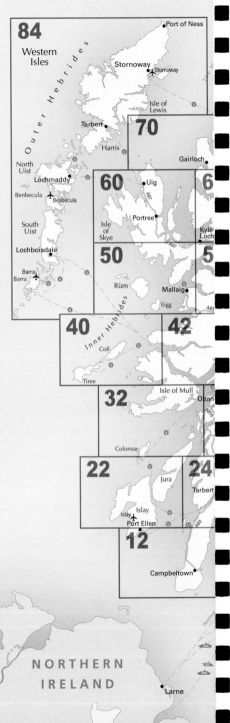

84 Western Isles   Port of Ness   Stornoway   Isle of Lewis   **70**   Gairloch   **60**   **6**   Uig   Tarbert   Harris   North Uist   Lochmaddy   Benbecula   Portree   Kyle Loch   South Uist   Isle of Skye   **50**   **5**   Lochboisdale   Barra   Rùm   Mallaig   **40**   **42**   Eigg   Coll   Isle of Mull   Tiree   **32**   Oban   Colonsay   **22**   **24**   Jura   Tarbert   Islay   Port Ellen   **12**   Campbeltown   NORTHERN IRELAND   Larne   BELFAST   Outer Hebrides   Inner Hebrides

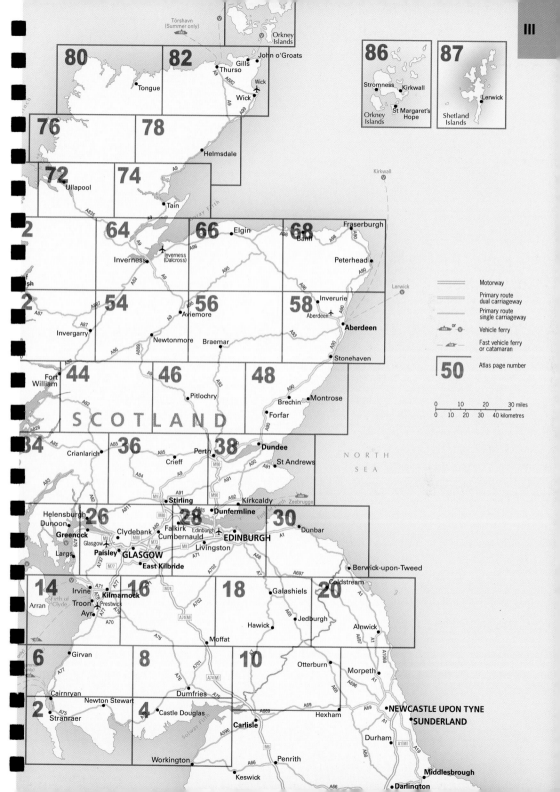

80 Tongue

82 Gills, Thurso, John o'Groats, Wick

86 Stromness, Kirkwall, St Margaret's Hope, Orkney Islands

87 Lerwick, Shetland Islands

Tórshavn (Summer only)

Orkney Islands

76

78 Helmsdale

72 Ullapool

74 Tain

Kirkwall

2

64 Inverness, Inverness (Dalcross)

66 Elgin

68 Fraserburgh, Banff, Peterhead

2

54 Aviemore

56 Newtonmore, Braemar

58 Inverurie, Aberdeen, Stonehaven

Lerwick

44 Fort William

46 Pitlochry

48 Brechin, Montrose, Forfar

S C O T L A N D

34 Crianlarich

36 Crieff

38 Perth, Dundee, St Andrews

Kirkcaldy

N O R T H   S E A

Zeebrugge

26 Helensburgh, Dunoon, Greenock, Largs, Paisley, GLASGOW, Clydebank, East Kilbride

Stirling

28 Dunfermline, Falkirk, Cumbernauld, Edinburgh, EDINBURGH, Livingston

30 Dunbar

Berwick-upon-Tweed

14 Irvine, Troon, Ayr, Prestwick, Arran, Kilmarnock

16

18 Galashiels, Hawick, Jedburgh

Coldstream

20 Alnwick

6 Girvan

8

10 Otterburn

Morpeth

2 Stranraer, Cairnryan, Newton Stewart

4 Dumfries, Castle Douglas

Carlisle, Hexham

NEWCASTLE UPON TYNE, SUNDERLAND

Durham

Moffat

Workington, Penrith, Keswick

Middlesbrough, Darlington

Legend

Motorway	
Primary route dual carriageway	
Primary route single carriageway	
Vehicle ferry	or
Fast vehicle ferry or catamaran	
50 Atlas page number	

0   10   20   30 miles
0 10 20 30 40 kilometres

Map pages

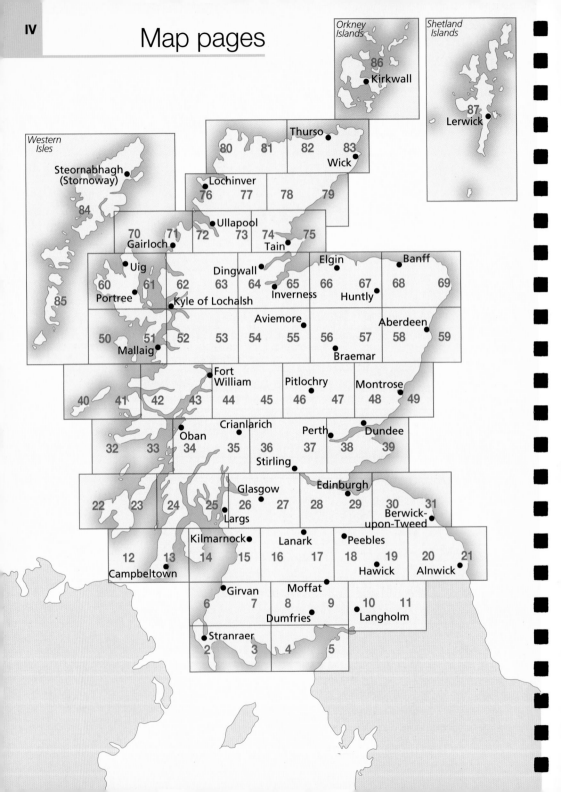

Orkney Islands
86 Kirkwall

Shetland Islands
87 Lerwick

Western Isles
Steornabhagh (Stornoway)
84
85

Thurso
80 81 82 83
Wick

Lochinver
76 77 78 79

Ullapool
70 71 72 73 74 75
Gairloch Tain

Uig
Elgin Banff
Dingwall
60 61 62 63 64 65 66 67 68 69
Portree Inverness Huntly
Kyle of Lochalsh

Aviemore Aberdeen
50 51 52 53 54 55 56 57 58 59
Mallaig Braemar

Fort William Pitlochry Montrose
40 41 42 43 44 45 46 47 48 49

Crianlarich Dundee
Oban Perth
32 33 34 35 36 37 38 39
Stirling

Glasgow Edinburgh
22 23 24 25 26 27 28 29 30 31
Largs Berwick-upon-Tweed

Kilmarnock Lanark Peebles
12 13 14 15 16 17 18 19 20 21
Campbeltown Hawick Alnwick

Girvan Moffat
6 7 8 9 10 11
Dumfries Langholm

Stranraer
2 3 4 5

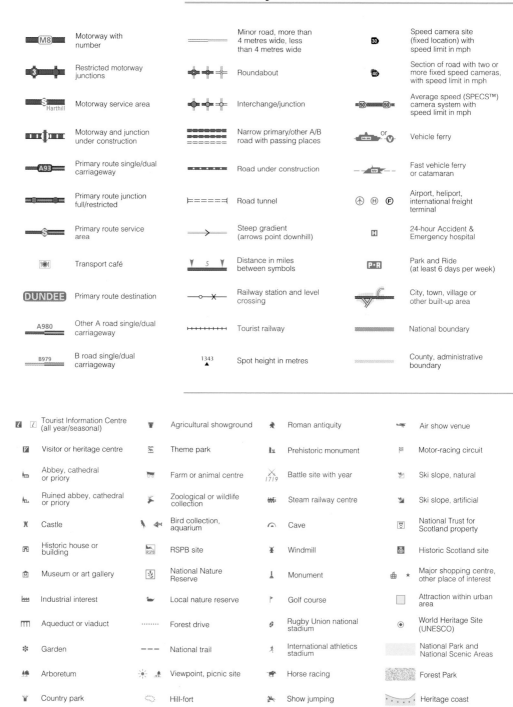

M8 Motorway with number

3 Restricted motorway junctions

S Harthill — Motorway service area

Motorway and junction under construction

A93 Primary route single/dual carriageway

Primary route junction full/restricted

S Primary route service area

Transport café

DUNDEE Primary route destination

A980 Other A road single/dual carriageway

B979 B road single/dual carriageway

Minor road, more than 4 metres wide, less than 4 metres wide

Roundabout

Interchange/junction

Narrow primary/other A/B road with passing places

Road under construction

Road tunnel

Steep gradient (arrows point downhill)

Distance in miles between symbols

Railway station and level crossing

Tourist railway

1343 Spot height in metres

30 Speed camera site (fixed location) with speed limit in mph

40 Section of road with two or more fixed speed cameras, with speed limit in mph

50 **50** Average speed (SPECS™) camera system with speed limit in mph

or **V** Vehicle ferry

Fast vehicle ferry or catamaran

Airport, heliport, international freight terminal

H 24-hour Accident & Emergency hospital

P•R Park and Ride (at least 6 days per week)

City, town, village or other built-up area

National boundary

County, administrative boundary

Tourist Information Centre (all year/seasonal)

Visitor or heritage centre

Abbey, cathedral or priory

Ruined abbey, cathedral or priory

Castle

Historic house or building

Museum or art gallery

Industrial interest

Aqueduct or viaduct

Garden

Arboretum

Country park

Agricultural showground

Theme park

Farm or animal centre

Zoological or wildlife collection

Bird collection, aquarium

RSPB site

National Nature Reserve

Local nature reserve

Forest drive

National trail

Viewpoint, picnic site

Hill-fort

Roman antiquity

Prehistoric monument

Battle site with year

Steam railway centre

Cave

Windmill

Monument

Golf course

Rugby Union national stadium

International athletics stadium

Horse racing

Show jumping

Air show venue

Motor-racing circuit

Ski slope, natural

Ski slope, artificial

National Trust for Scotland property

Historic Scotland site

Major shopping centre, other place of interest

Attraction within urban area

World Heritage Site (UNESCO)

National Park and National Scenic Areas

Forest Park

Heritage coast

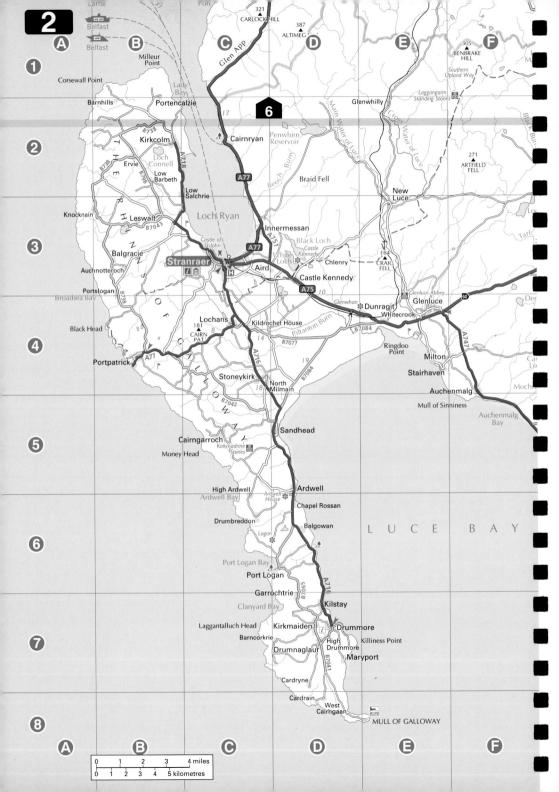

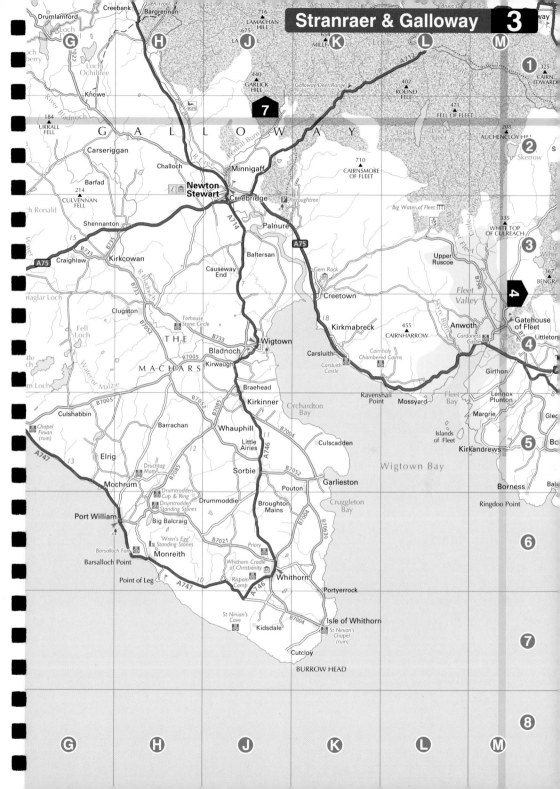

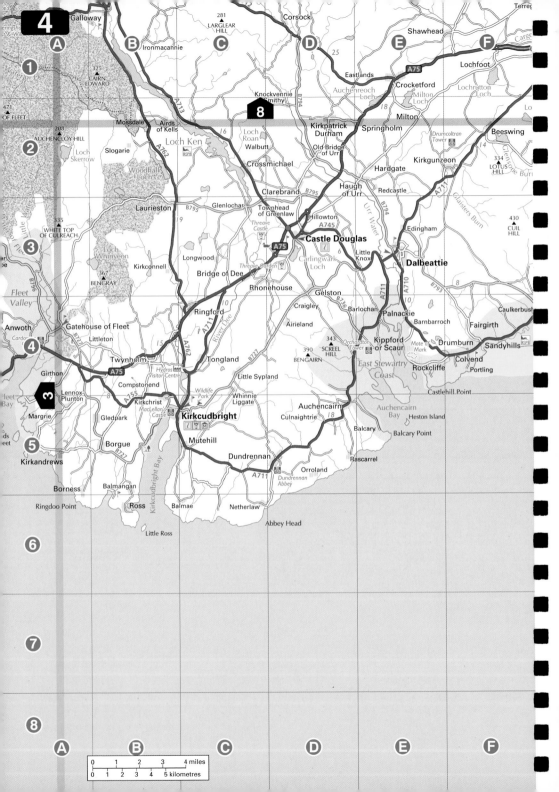

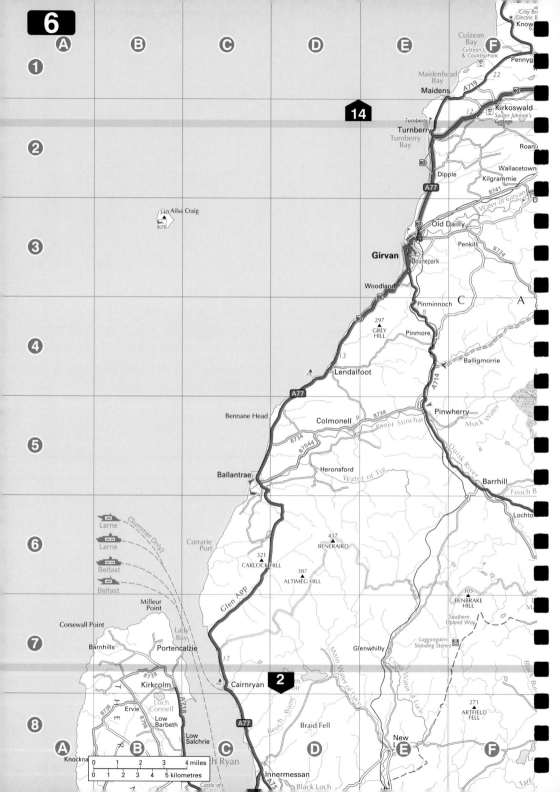

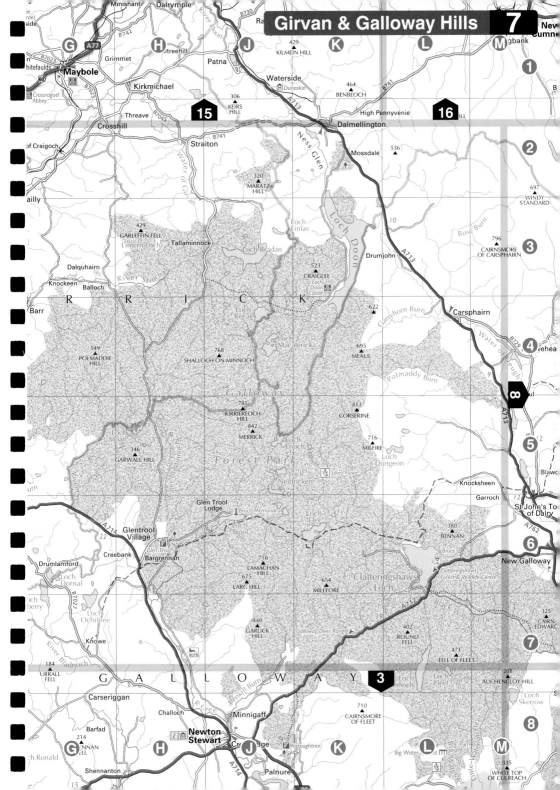

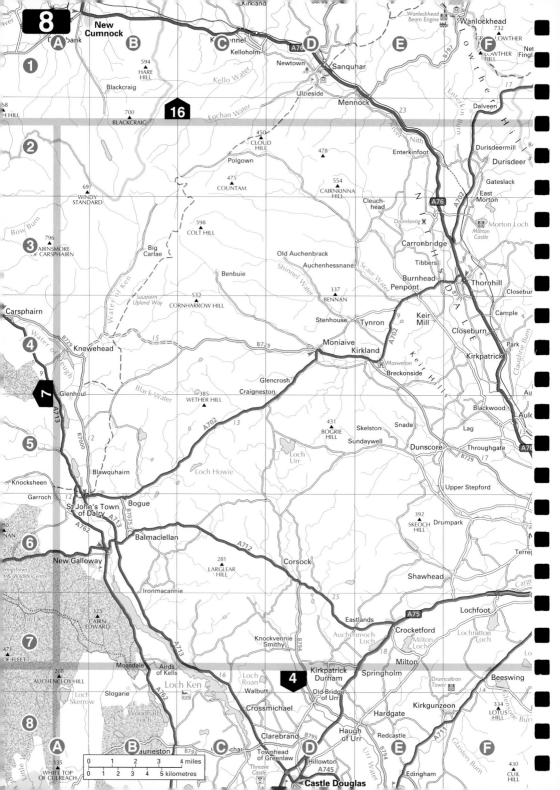

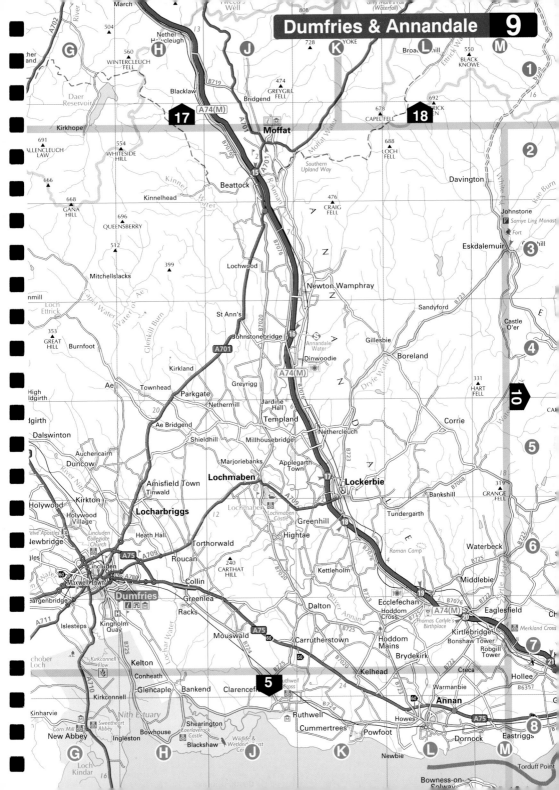

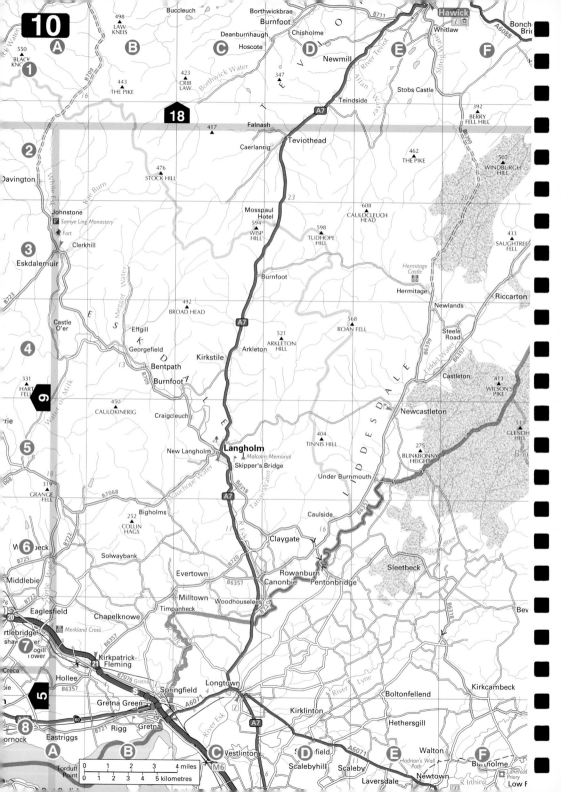

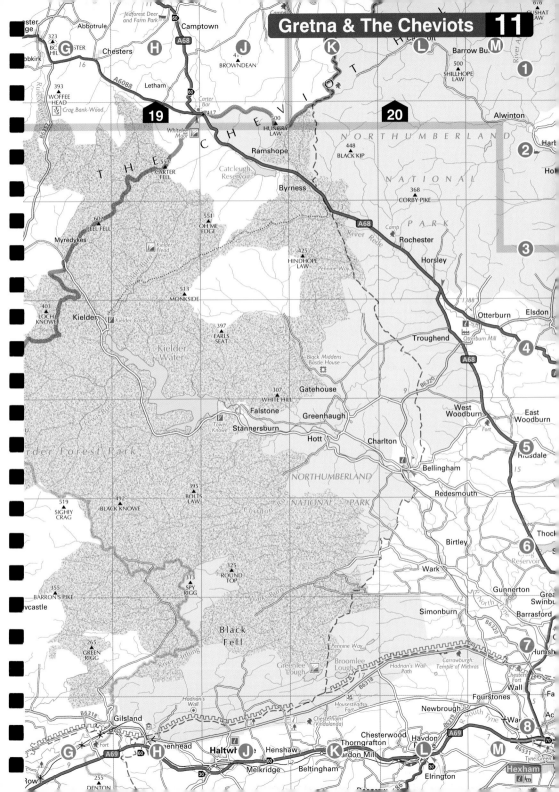

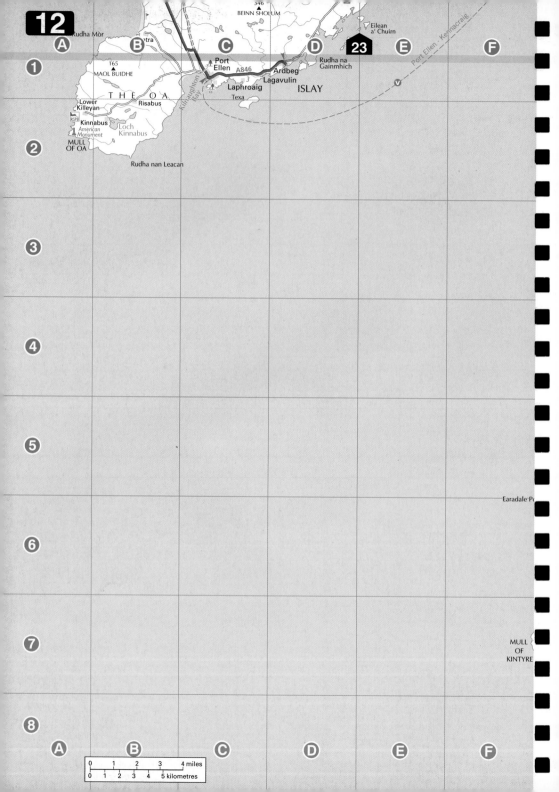

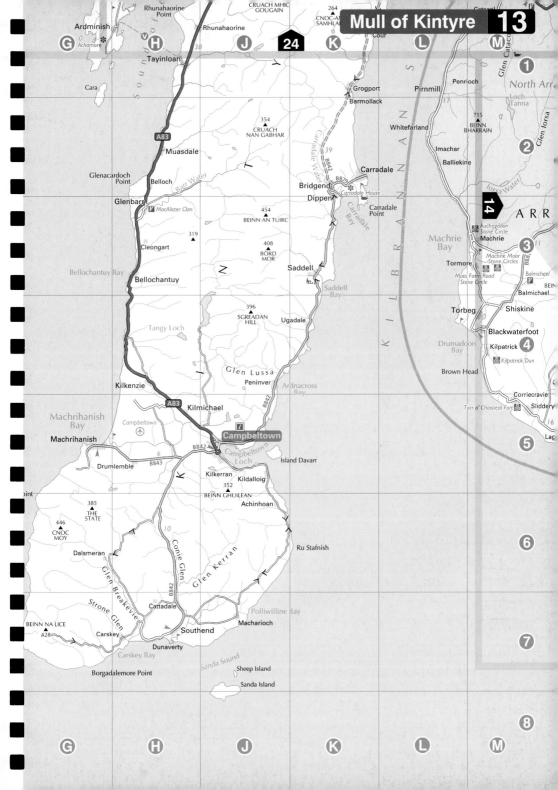

G · H · J · **24** · K · L · M

Rhunahaorine Point
Ardminish
Achamore
Tayinloan
Cara
Rhunahaorine

Grogport
Barmollack
Cour

Pirnmill
Penrioch
North Arr
Loch Tanna

CRUACH MHIC GOUGAIN
CNOC-AN-SAMHLA
264

354
CRUACH NAN GABHAR

Carradale Water
B842

Whitefarland

715
BEINN BHARRAIN

Imachar
Balliekine

Torsa Water

A83
Muasdale

Glenacardoch Point
Belloch

Carradale
B879
Bridgend
Dippen
Carradale House
Carradale Point

Machrie Bay
Auchagallon Stone Circle
Machrie

ARR

ARRAN

Glenbarr
MacAlister Clan

454
BEINN AN TUIRC

Saddell

Carradale Bay

Carradale Point

Tormore
Machrie Moor Stone Circles
Moss Farm Road Stone Circle

3

BEINN
Balmichael
Balmichael

319

Cleongart

408
BORD MOR

Saddell Bay

Shiskine

Bellochantuy Bay
Bellochantuy

Z

396
SGREADAN HILL

Ugadale

Torbeg

Blackwaterfoot
Kilpatrick

4

Drumadoon Bay

Kilpatrick Dun

Brown Head

Tangy Loch

Glen Lussa
Peninver

Ardnacross Bay

Corriecravie
Sliddery

Kilkenzie

A83
Kilmichael

B842

Torr a' Chaisteal Fort

5

La

Machrihanish Bay
Machrihanish

Campbeltown
Campbeltown

Campbeltown Loch
Island Davarr

B842
B843

Drumlemble

6

385
THE STATE

Kilkerran
Kildalloig

352
BEINN GHUILEAN

Achinhoan

6

446
CNOC MOY

Dalsmeran

Glen Kerran

Ru Stafnish

Conie Glen

Glen Breakevie

B842

Cattadale

Polliwilline Bay

Strone Glen

7

BEINN NA LICE
428
Carskey

Southend
Dunaverty

Macharioch

Carskey Bay

Borgadalemore Point

Sanda Sound
Sheep Island

Sanda Island

8

G · H · J · K · L · M

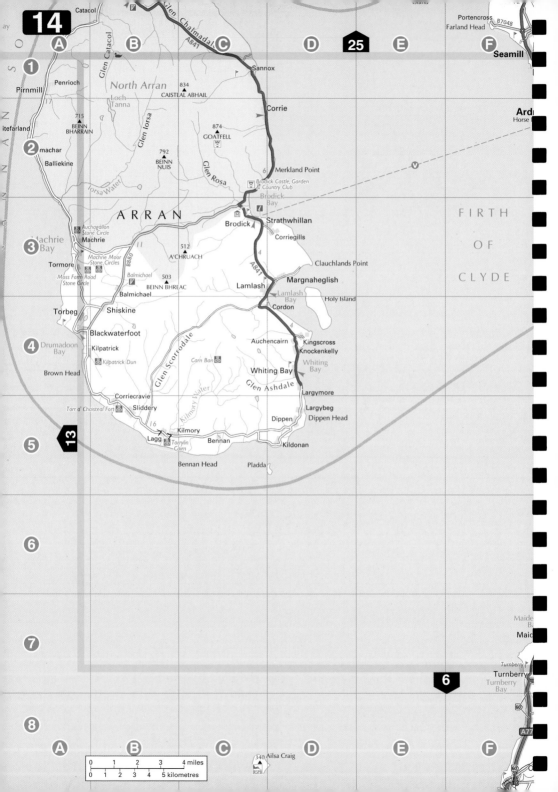

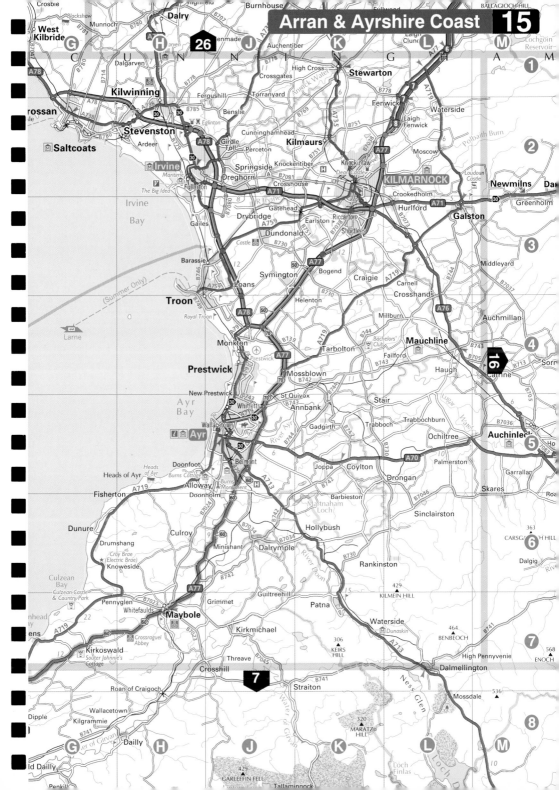

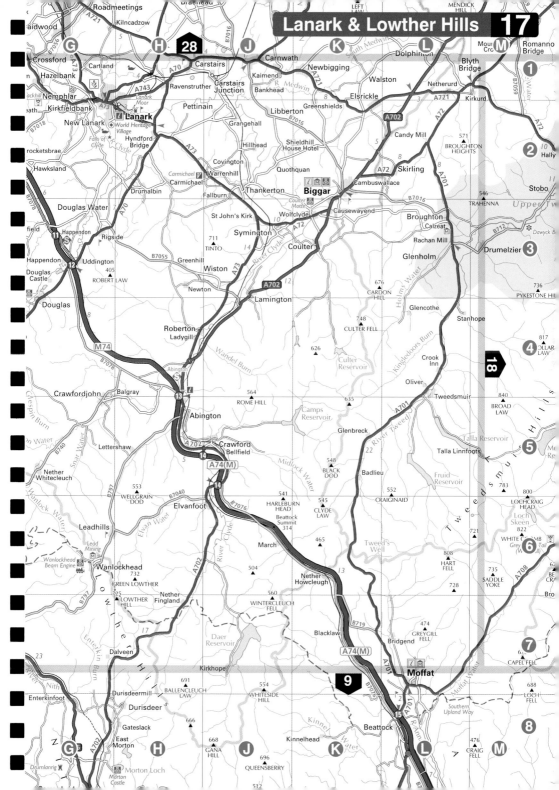

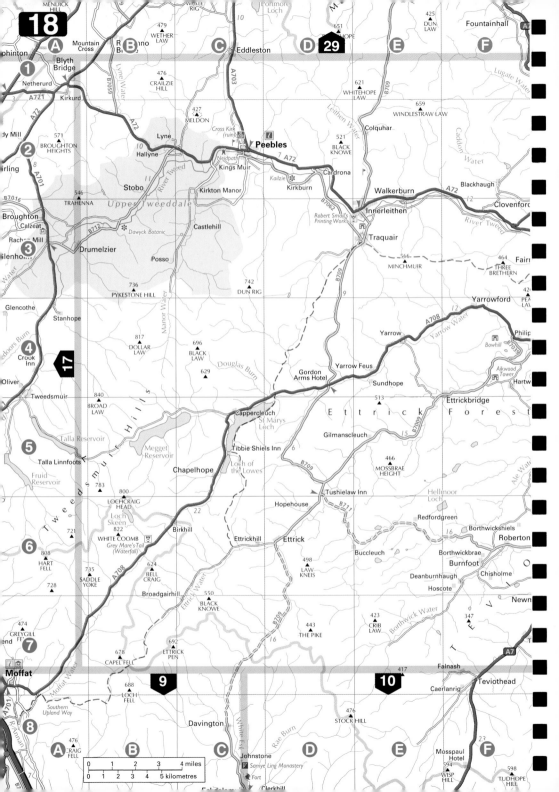

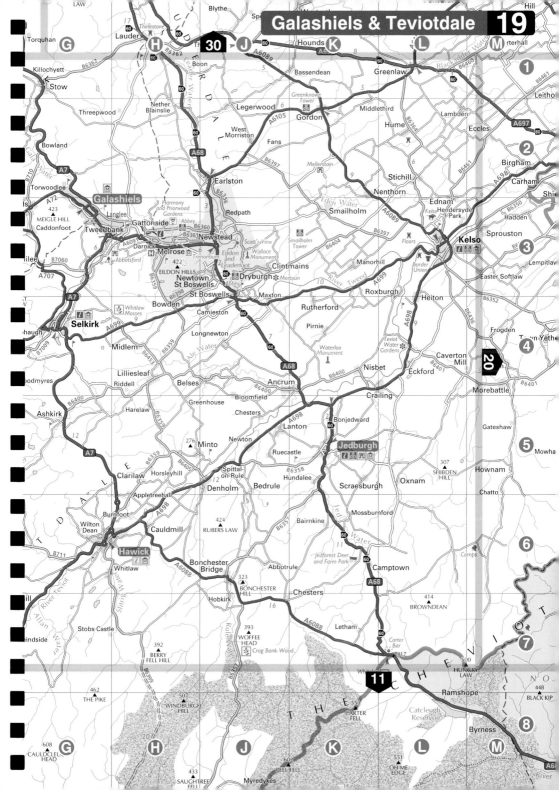

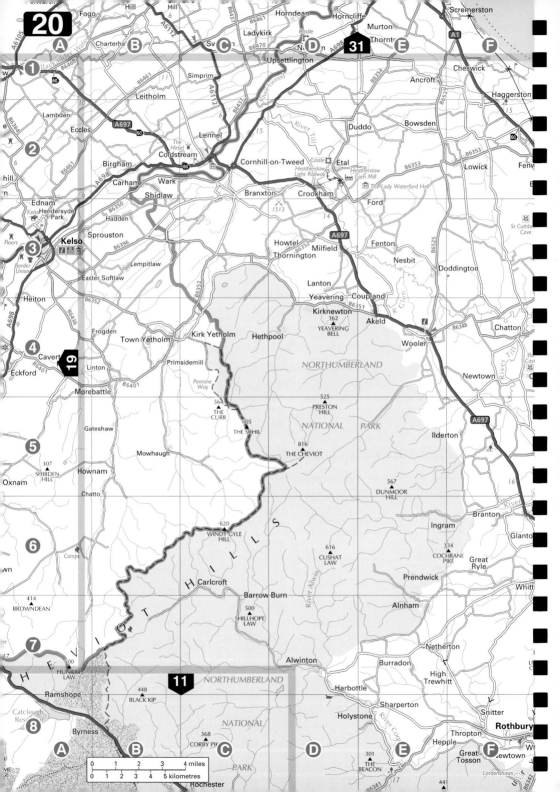

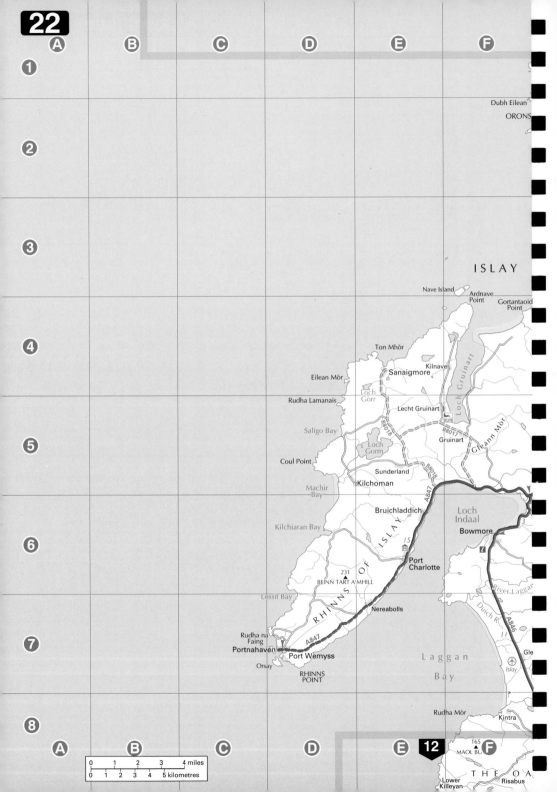

A   B   C   D   E   F

1

2

Dubh Eilean

ORONS

3

ISLAY

Nave Island   Ardnave
Point   Gortantaoid
Point

4   Ton Mhòr

Kilnave

Sanaigmore

Eilean Mòr

Loch
Gorr   Loch
Gruinart

Rudha Lamanais   Lecht Gruinart   B8017

Gleann Mòr

Saligo Bay

5   Loch
Gorm   Gruinart

Coul Point   Sunderland

Kilchoman   A847

Machir
Bay   Loch
Indaal

Bruichladdich

Kilchiaran Bay   Bowmore

6   RHINNS   Port
Charlotte

231
BEINN TART A'MHILL   River Laggan

Lossit Bay   OF   Duich R.   A846

RHINNS   Nereabolls

7   Rudha na
Faing   ISLAY   A847

Portnahaven   Islay   Gle

Port Wemyss

Orsay   Laggan

RHINNS
POINT   Bay

8   Rudha Mòr   Kintra

A   B   C   D   E   **12**   165
MAOL BU   F

THE OA

0   1   2   3   4 miles
0   1   2   3   4   5 kilometres

Lower
Killeyan   Risabus

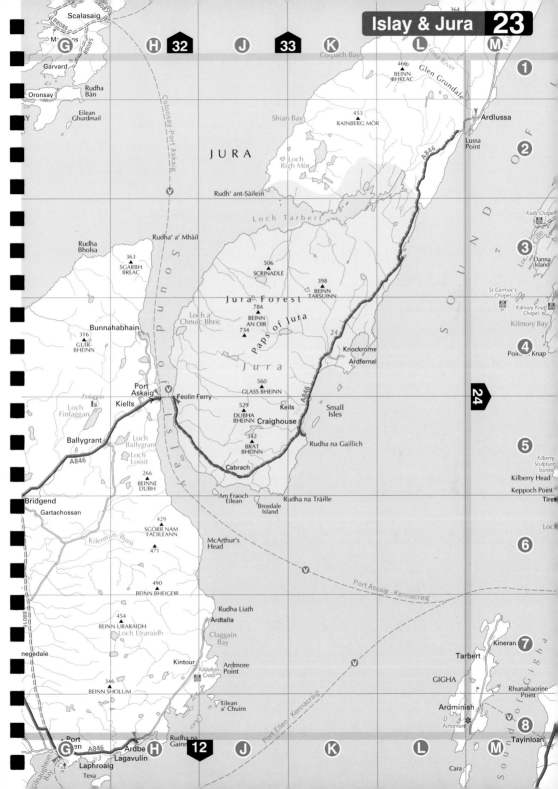

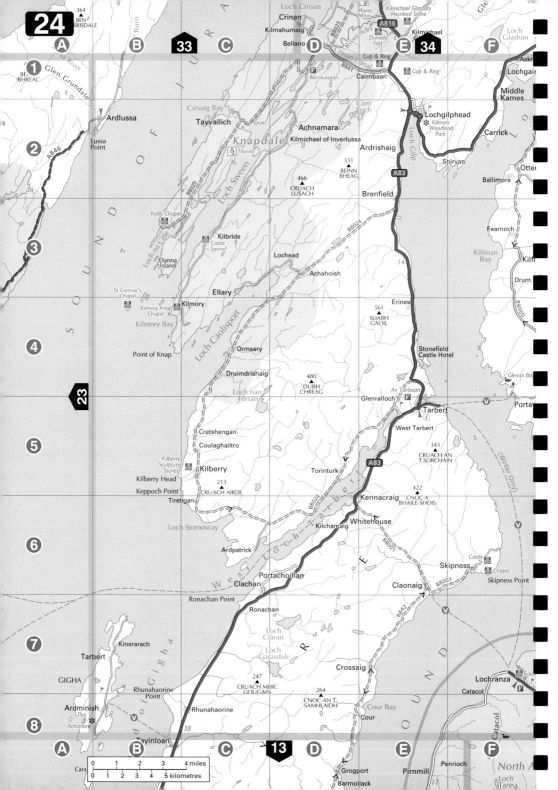

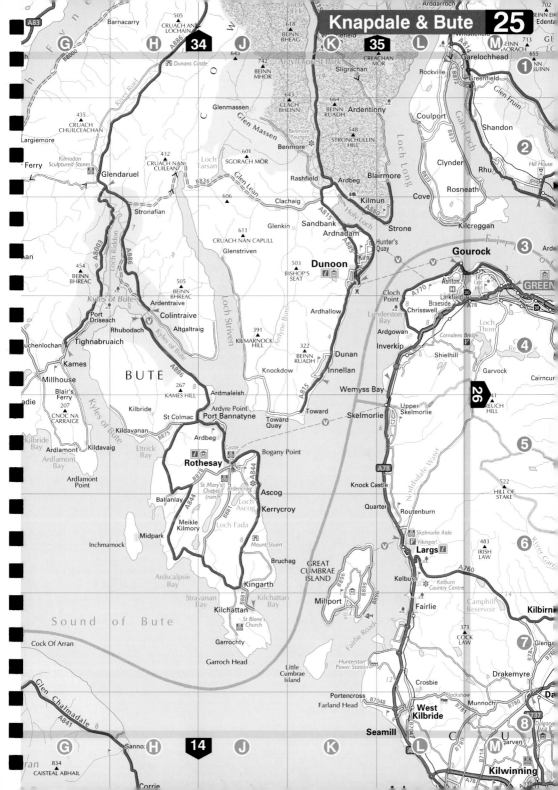

Barnacarry

A83

G   H   A886   34   J   K   35   L   M

702

Arddarroch
Edenta

505
CRUACH AN
LOCHAIN

643

618
BEINN
BHEAG

Whitefield

CREACHAN
MOR

Whistlefield

713
BEINN EIN
NAORACH

655
NN SUINN

Garelochhead

Dunans Castle

742
BEINN
MHOR

Argyll Forest Park

Sligrachan

Rockville

Greenfield

Glen Fruin

1

435
CRUACH
CHUILCEACHAN

Glenmassen

643
CLACH
BHEINN

664
BEINN
RUADH

Ardentinny

Coulport

Shandon

Largiemore

Benmore

Benmore
Younger

548
STRONCHULLIN
HILL

Clynder

Rhu

Hill House

2

Ferry

Kilmodan
Sculptured Stones

432
CRUACH NAN
CUILEAN

Loch
Tarsan

601
SGORACH MOR

Rashfield

Ardbeg

Blairmore

Loch Long

B833

Cove

Rosneath

Kilcreggan

Glendaruel

B836

Glen Lean

606

Clachaig

Kilmun

A880

Holy Loch

Strone

Stronafian

611
CRUACH NAN CAPULL

Glenkin

Sandbank

Ardnadam

Hunter's
Quay

Gourock

454
BEINN
BHREAC

A886

Loch Kiddon

A8003

Glenstriven

503
BISHOP'S
SEAT

Dunoon

Kirn

Lunderston
Bay

Ashton

Lye

GREEN

3

Ard

505
BEINN
BHREAC

Ardentraive

Colintraive

Loch Striven

391
KILMARNOCK
HILL

Ardyne Burn

Ardhallow

Cloch
Point

Braeside

Chrisswell

A78

30

Port
Driseach

Rhubodach

Altgaltraig

322
BEINN
RUADH

Dunan

Ardgowan

Inverkip

Shielhill

Loch
Thom

4

Garvock

Cairncur

uchenlochan

Tighnabruaich

Kyles of Bute

A886

Knockdow

Innellan

Cornalees Bridge

Kames

BUTE

267
8
KAMES HILL

Ardmaleish

Wemyss Bay

Upper
Skelmorlie

522
HILL OF
STAKE

5

Millhouse

Blair's
Ferry

Kilbride

Ardyre Point

Toward
Quay

Skelmorlie

26

41
REUCH
HILL

adie

207
CNOC NA
CARRAIGE

Kildavanan

St Colmac

Port Bannatyne

Ardbeg

Toward

Noddsdale Water

Kilbride
Bay

Ardlamont

Kildavaig

B875

Castle

Bogany Point

Knock Castle

483
IRISH
LAW

6

Ardlamont
Bay

Rothesay

Quarter

Routenburn

Ardlamont
Point

Ettrick
Bay

St Mary's
Chapel
(ruin)

Ardencraig

Ascog

Kerrycroy

A78

Skelmorlie Aisle

Vikingar!

Largs

Kelburn
Country Centre

Camphill
Reservoir

Kilbirni

Ballanlay

A844

Meikle
Kilmory

Loch
Ascog

Loch Fada

Mount Stuart

Kelburn

Fairlie

371
COCK
LAW

7

Glenga

Inchmarnock

Midpark

Bruchag

GREAT
CUMBRAE
ISLAND

B78

Drakemyre

Ardscalpsie
Bay

Kingarth

B881

Kilchattan
Bay

Millport

Little
Cumbrae
Island

Fairlie
Roads

Crosbie

Munnoch

B780

8

Da

Strayanan
Bay

Kilchattan

St Blane's
Church

Hunterston
Power Station

Portencross

B7048

Farland Head

**West
Kilbride**

Blackshaw

B781

Sound of Bute

Garrochty

Seamill

B714

Cock Of Arran

Garroch Head

A78

G   H   14   J   K   L   M

834
CAISTEAL ABHAIL

Sanno

Glen Chalmadale

A841

8

Corrie

Kilwinning

garven

N

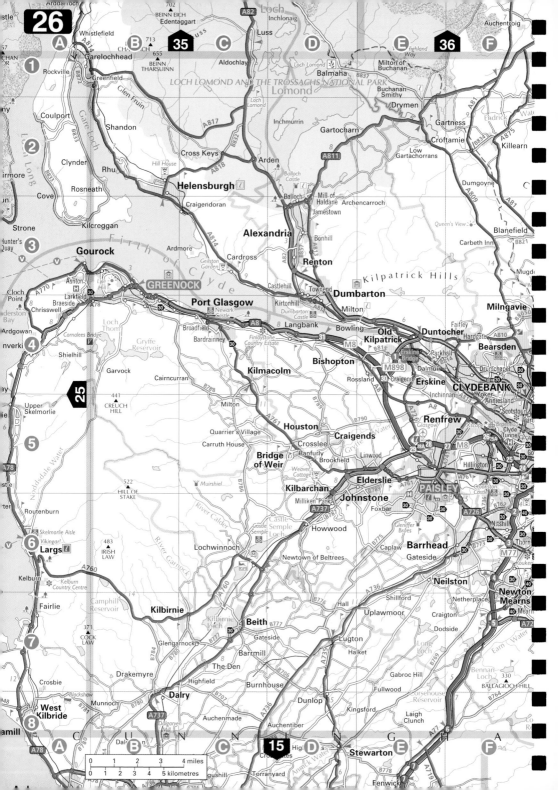

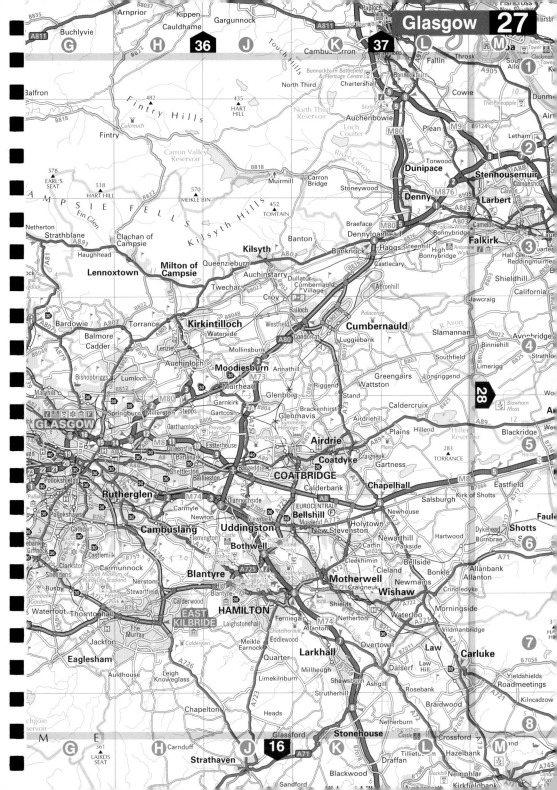

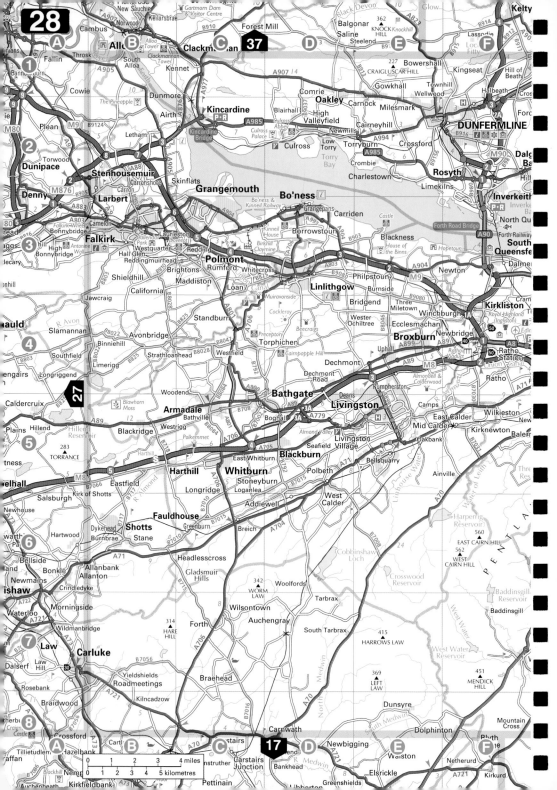

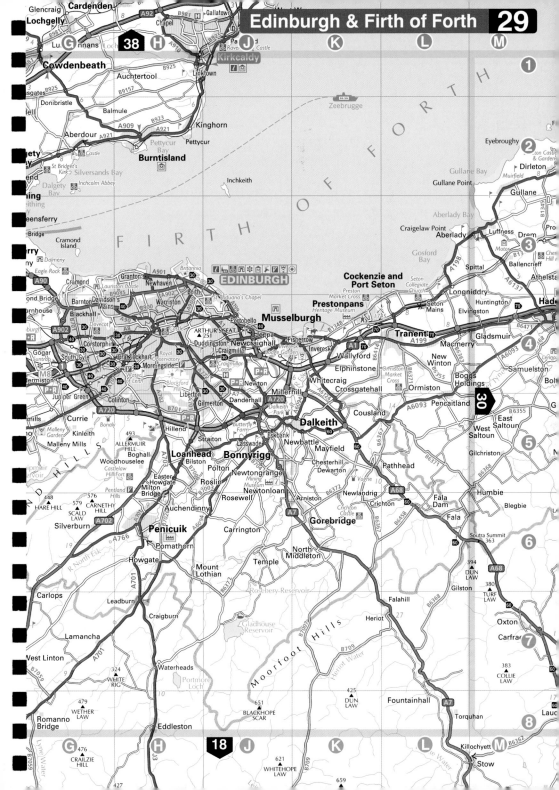

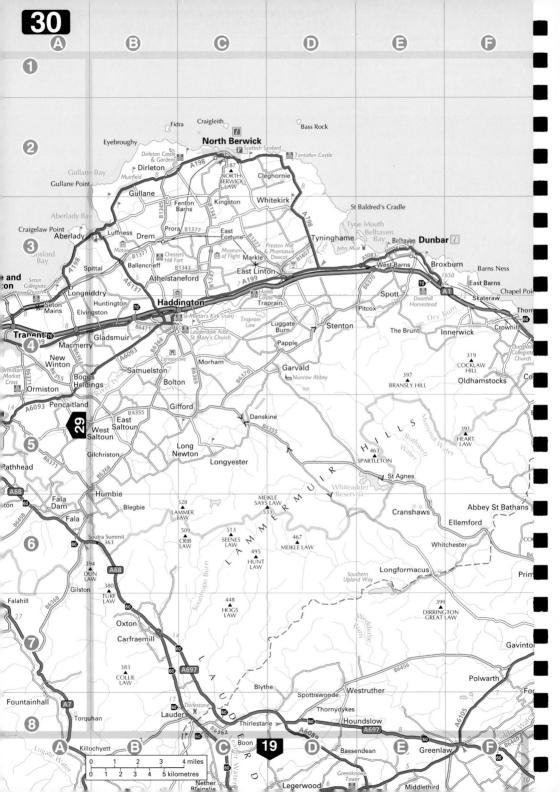

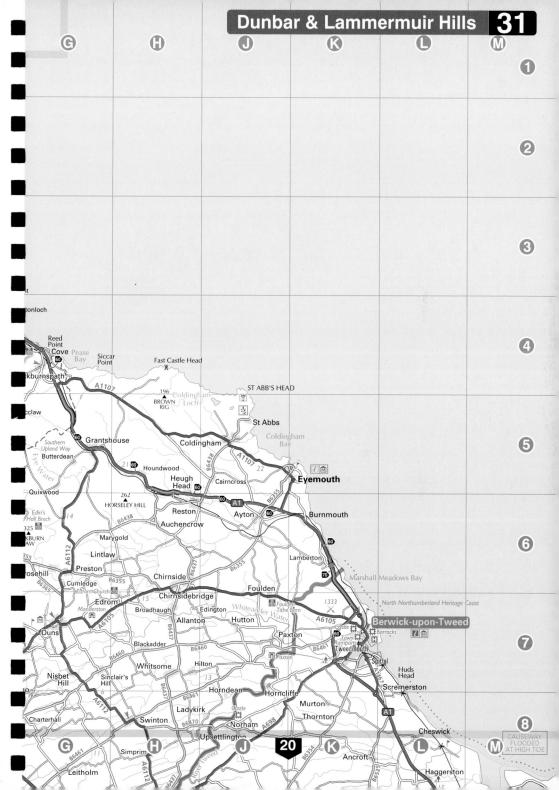

G H J K L M

1 2 3 4 5 6 7 8

Reed Point
Cove
Pease Bay
Siccar Point
Fast Castle Head
kburnspath
A1107
ST ABB'S HEAD
196
BROWN RIG
Coldingham Loch
St Abbs
cclaw
Grantshouse
Coldingham
Coldingham Bay
Southern Upland Way
Butterdean
Houndwood
A1107 22
Eyemouth
21 60
B6438
Quixwood
HEUGH HEAD
Heugh Head
Cairncross
262
HORSELEY HILL
A1
Edin's Hall Broch
14
Reston
Ayton 60
Burnmouth
325
KBURN AW
355
B6438
Auchencrow
B6355
A6112
Marygold
B6437
B6355
Lamberton
60
Lintlaw
70
Marshall Meadows Bay
osehill
Preston
B6365
Cumledge
B6355
Chirnside
Foulden
North Northumberland Heritage Coast
Edrom
Chirnsidebridge
1333
A6105
Manderston
Broadhaugh
Edington
Whiteadder Water
Foulden Tithe Barn
Berwick-upon-Tweed
Allanton
Hutton
Barracks
Duns
A6105
B6437
Paxton
Town Ramparts
60
Blackadder
B6460
Hilton
B6461
Tweedmouth
Nisbet Hill
Whitsome
Paxton
Spittal
Sinclair's Hill
13
Huds Head
Charterhall
A6112
6
Horndean
Horncliffe
Murton
Scremerston
Ladykirk
Thornton
A1
Swinton
B6470
Castle
Norham A698
Cheswick
CAUSEWAY FLOODED AT HIGH TIDE

G H J **20** K L M

B6461
Simprim
B6554
Ancroft
Leitholm
River Tweed
Upsettlington
Haggerston

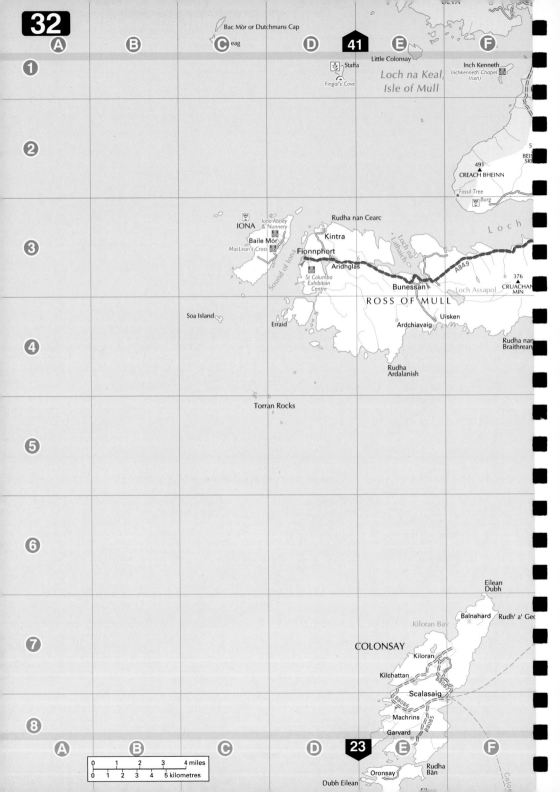

1

Bac Mòr or Dutchmans Cap

eag

Staffa

Little Colonsay

Inch Kenneth

Inchkenneth Chapel (ruin)

Loch na Keal,
Isle of Mull

Fingal's Cave

2

491
CREACH BHEINN

BEIN
SRI

Fossil Tree

Burg

3

Rudha nan Cearc

IONA

Iona Abbey
& Nunnery

Kintra

Loch na Latnaich

Loch

Baile Mòr

MacLean's Cross

Fionnphort

Aridhglas

St Columba
Exhibition
Centre

Bunessan

Loch Assapol

A849

376
CRUACHAN
MIN

ROSS OF MULL

Sound of Iona

4

Soa Island

Erraid

Ardchiavaig

Uisken

Rudha nan
Braithrean

Rudha
Ardalanish

5

Torran Rocks

6

Eilean
Dubh

7

Balnahard

Rudh' a' Gec

Kiloran Bay

COLONSAY

Kiloran

Kilchattan

B8085

Scalasaig

B8085

B8086

Machrins

B8085

8

Garvard

0   1   2   3   4 miles
0 1 2 3 4 5 kilometres

Oronsay

Rudha
Bàn

Dubh Eilean

Colo

ISLE OF MULL

G H **42** J K L M **①**

Eorsa

BEINN NAN LUS

Macquarie Mausoleum

BEINN A' CHAIG

BEINN MHEADHON

Craignure

Mull & West Highland Narrow Gauge Railway

766 DUN DA GHAOITHE

Torosay Castle

Duart Bay Duart Point Duart

Kilcher

Rudha an Ridire

②

Calnahard

B8035

966 BEN MORE

704 CRUACHAN DEARG

Lochdonhead

Lochdon

Gorten

Aird of Kinloch

A849

Strathcoil

A849

Loch Don

Grass Point

KERRERA

19 NA NE

247 CÀRN BÀN

Pennycross

Pennyghael

698 BEN CREACH

717 BEN BUIE

Croggan

Rudha Seanach

③

Loch-Fuaran

Glen More

Loch Spelve

A849

503 BEINN NA CROISE

Lochbuie

Loch Uisg

337 MAOL BÀN

Barnacarry Bay

376 BEINN CHREAGACH

Carsaig

Rudha Dubh

377 DRUIM FADA

Loch Buie

FIRTH OF LORNE

Insh Island

Clachan-Seil

SEIL

Clachan

B844

Malcolm's Point

Ellanbeich

Easdale

Easdale

Balvicar

④

Cuan Ferry Village

Garbh Eileach

Cullipool House

Torsay Island

LUING

Sell Sound

Degnish

Loch Melfort

34

Garvellachs Monastery & Beehive Cells

Eilean Dubh Mòr

GARVELLACHS

Toberonochy

Arduaine Garden

Arduaine

⑤

Eileach an Naoimh

LUNGA

SHUNA

Craobh Haven

Ⓐ

Scarba, Lunga and the Garvellachs

Shuna Sound

Shuna Point

Craigdhu

SCARBA

448 CRUACH SCARBA

Ardfe

Kint

⑥

B8002

En Mhic

En Rig

Gulf of Corryvreckan

Aird

Glengarrisdale Bay

295 CRUACH NA SEILCHEIG

Craignish Point

Island Macaskin

Clockavulli Wood Circles

⑦

Ri Cruin Ca

Poltalloc

Glendebadel Bay

JURA

364 BEN GARRISDALE

Corpach Bay

Loch Crinan

Crinan

Kilmahumaig

Crinan River

Bellanoch

⑧

G H **23** J Glen Grundale K L **24** M

466 BEINN BHREAC

Lùssa River

Lealt Burn

JURA

Barnluasgan

Carsaig Bay

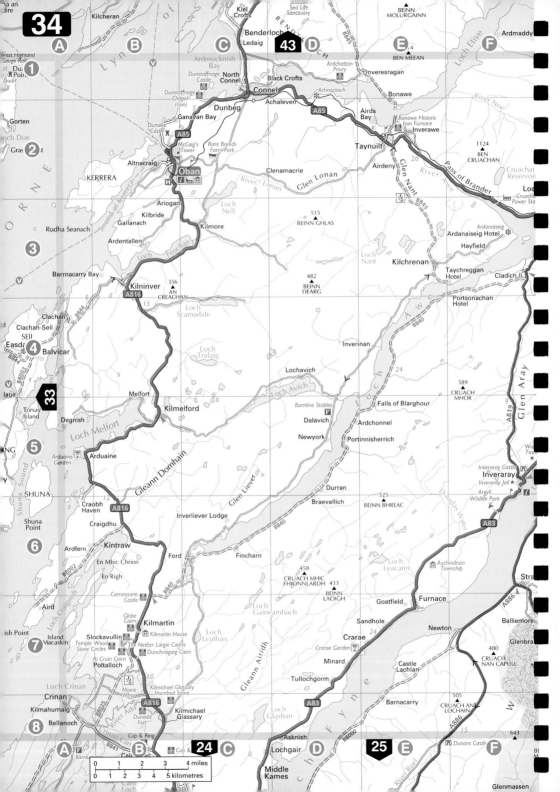

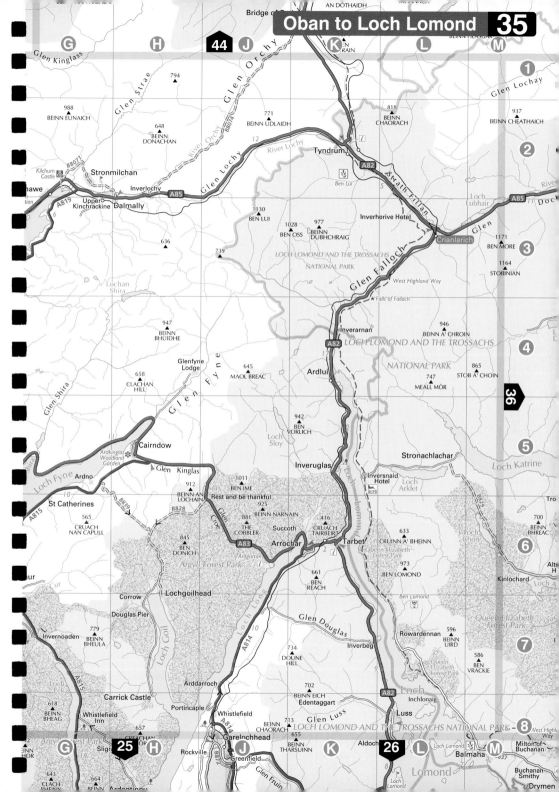

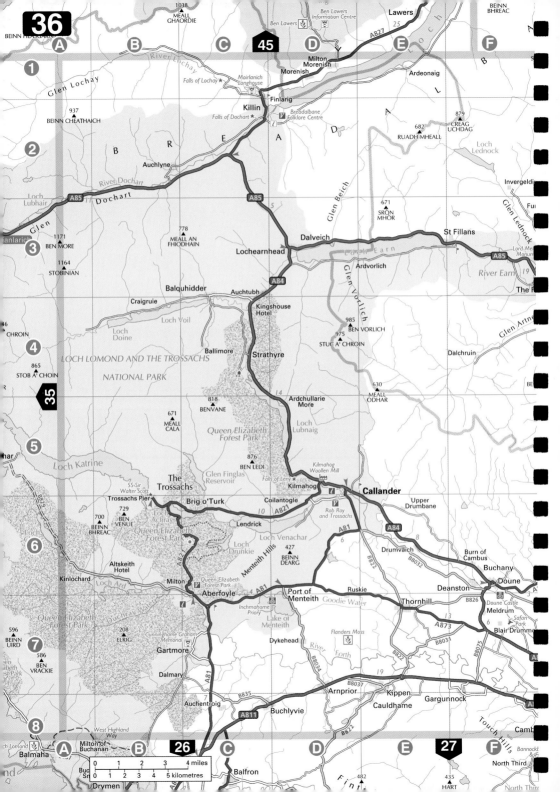

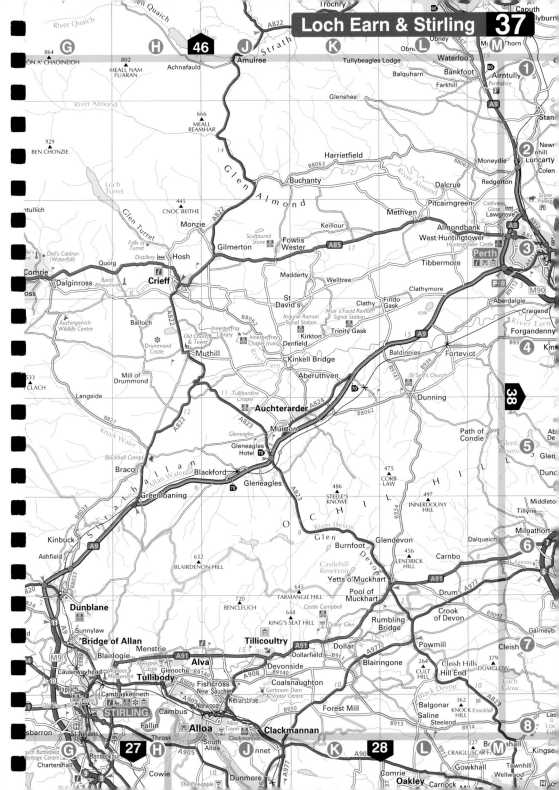

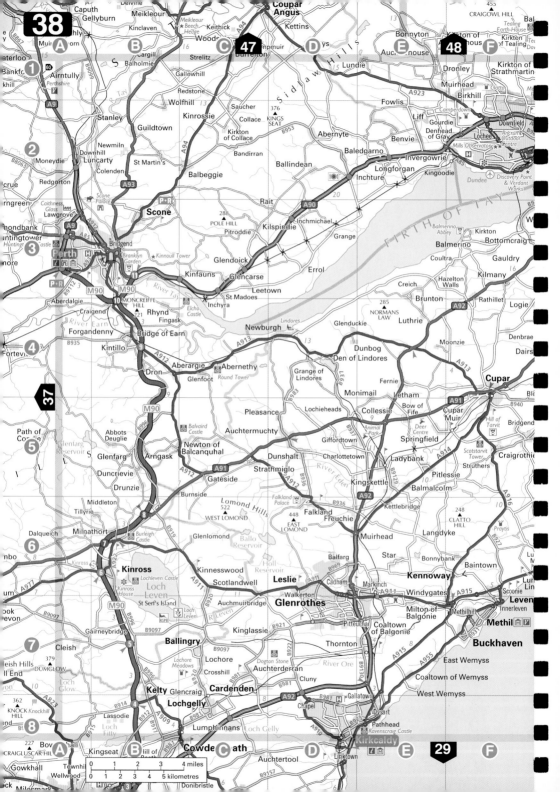

40

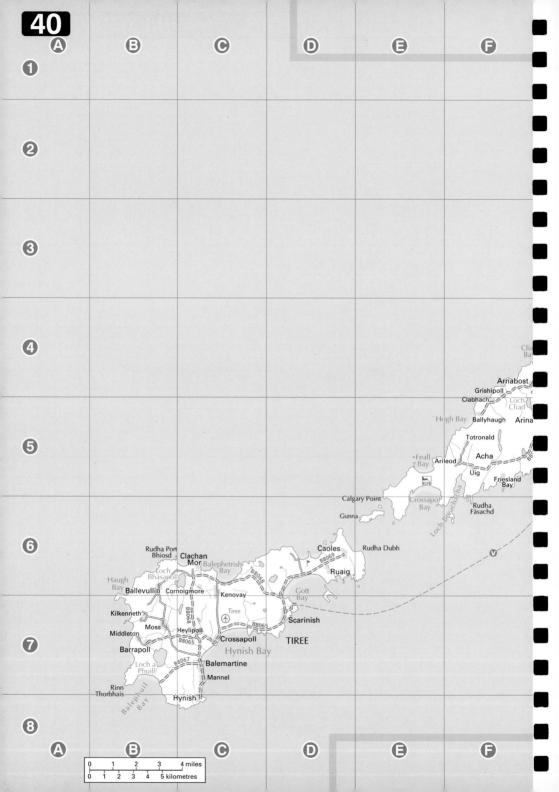

A B C D E F

1
2
3
4

Arnabost
Grishipoll
Clabhach
Loch Cliad
Hogh Bay Ballyhaugh Arina

5

Totronald
Feall Bay Arileod Acha
Uig
Friesland Bay
Calgary Point
Crossapol Bay
Gunna
Rudha Fàsachd

6

Rudha Port Bhiosd Clachan Mor Balephetrish Bay
Caoles Rudha Dubh
Ruaig
Haugh Bay Loch Bhasapoll
Ballevullin Cornoigmore Kenovay
Gott Bay
Kilkenneth Tiree
Moss Heylipoll
Middleton Scarinish
Crossapoll TIREE
Barrapoll Balemartine
Hynish Bay
Loch a Phuill
Mannel
Rinn Thorbhais
Hynish
Balephuill Bay

7
8

A B C D E F

0 1 2 3 4 miles
0 1 2 3 4 5 kilometres

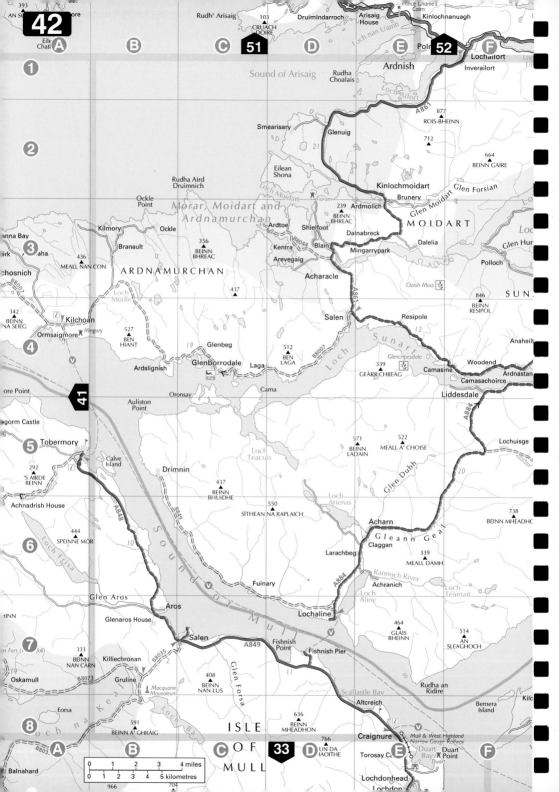

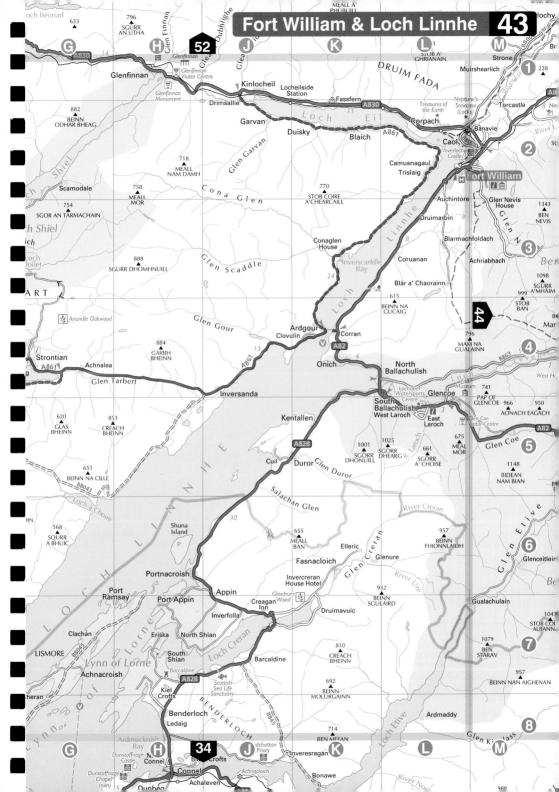

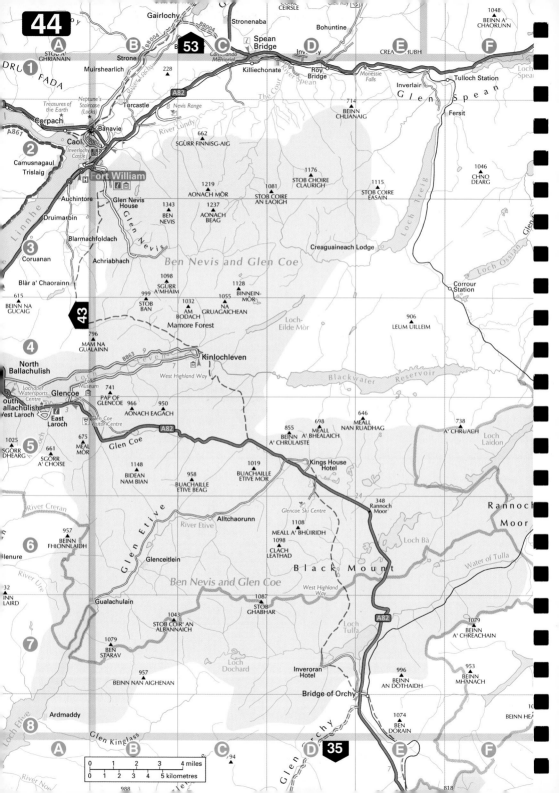

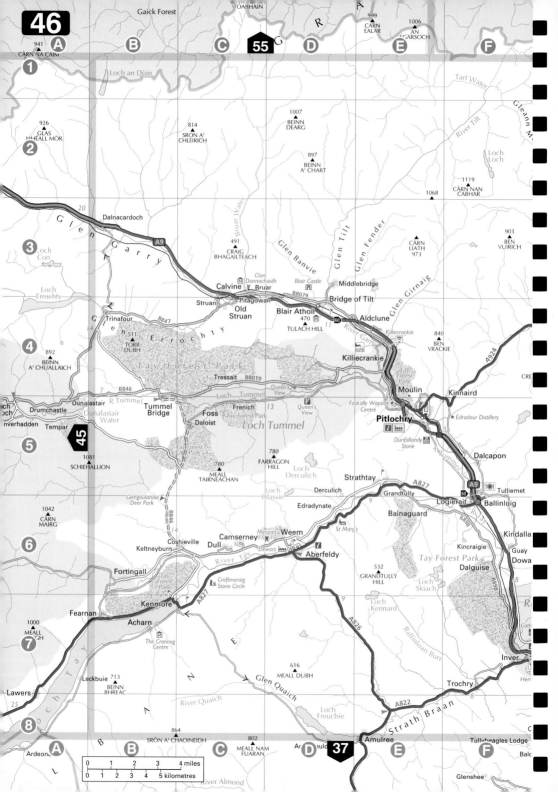

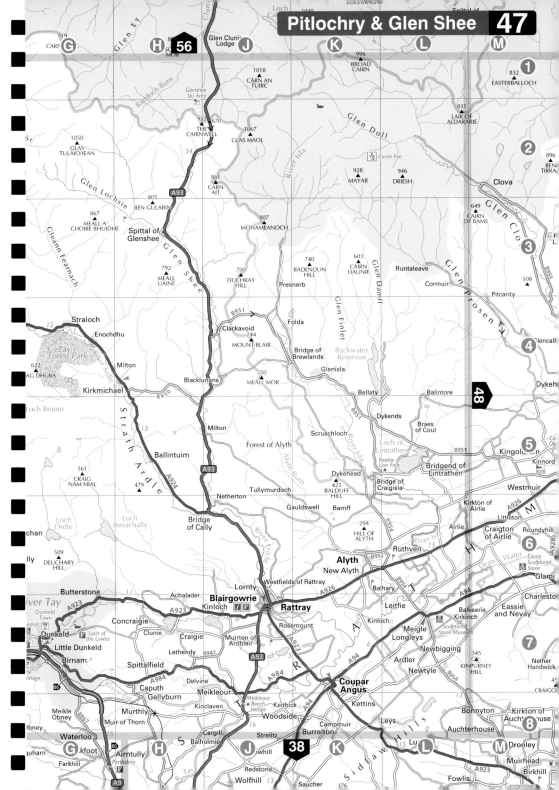

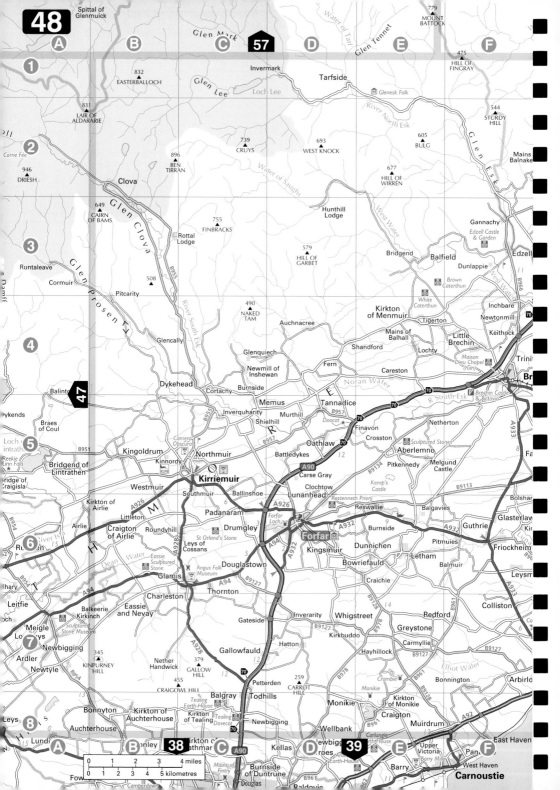

LEACHIE HILL
Tannachie
Goosecruives
58
v Mill
Drumlithie
Temple
of Fiddes
Crawton
Water of Dye
Glenbervie
Mondynes
Fowlsheugh
Trelong
Bay
465
GOYLE
HILL
454
Cairn
O'Mount
Catterline
Kinneff
Todhead Point
414
FINELLA
HILL
Auchenblae
Fasque
Fordoun
Arbuthnott
B966
Pittarrow
Redmyre
B967
Fettercairn
Inverbervie
Mains of
Haulkerton
B9120
Bogmuir
Laurencekirk
Bervie
Bay
Sauchieburn
Gourdon
B9120
Edzell
Woods
Redford
Luthermuir
Dykelands
Benholm
A90
North
Stracathro Hospital
Johnshaven
Logie Pert
Marykirk
Craigo
Lochside
Bush
Milton Ness
ty
Logie
Morphie
St Cyrus
Hillside
House of
Dun
echin
Dun
A935
Montrose
Montrose
Basin
Kinnaird
Castle
Barnhead
Scurdie Ness
Maryton
Ferryden
rnell
A934
Craig
Usan
Westerton
Boddin Point
132
WUDDY
LAW
Braehead
Lunan
Boysack
Lunan Bay
Inverkeilor
Red Head
Chapelton
Cauldcots
Letham
Grange
Marywell
St Vigeans
Auchmithie
Carlingheugh
Bay
The Deil's
Head
Arbroath

G H J K L M
① ② ③ ④ ⑤ ⑥ ⑦ ⑧

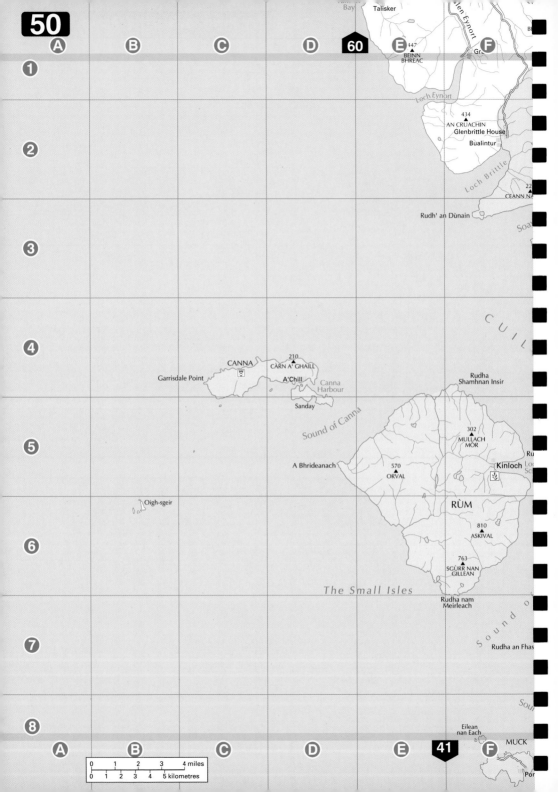

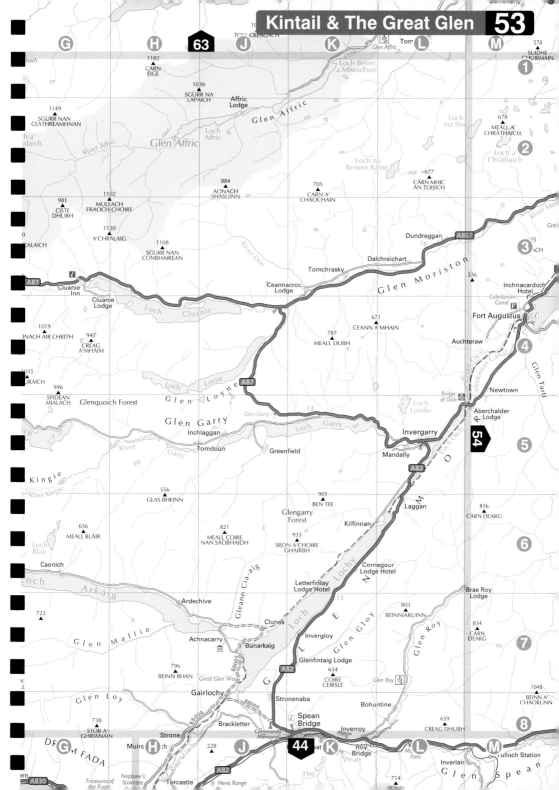

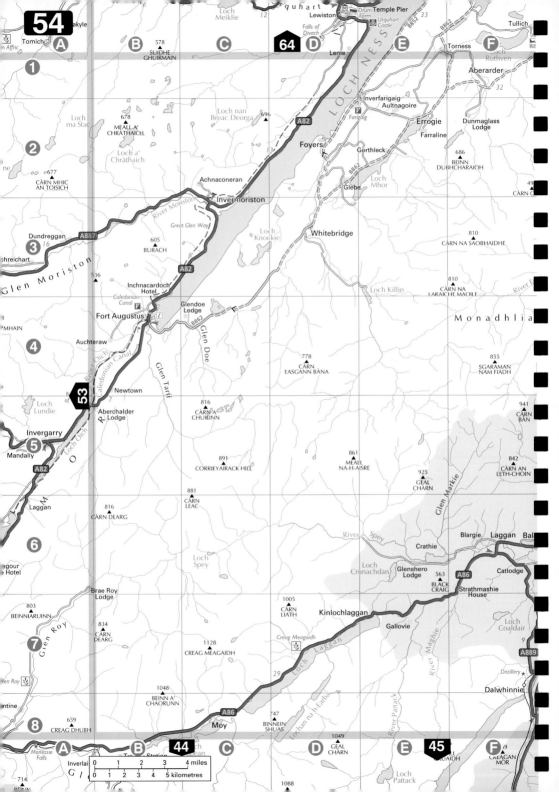

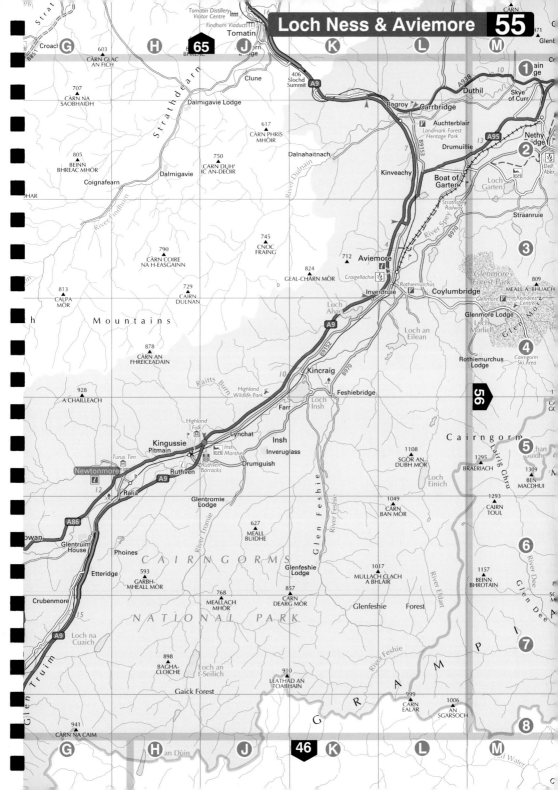

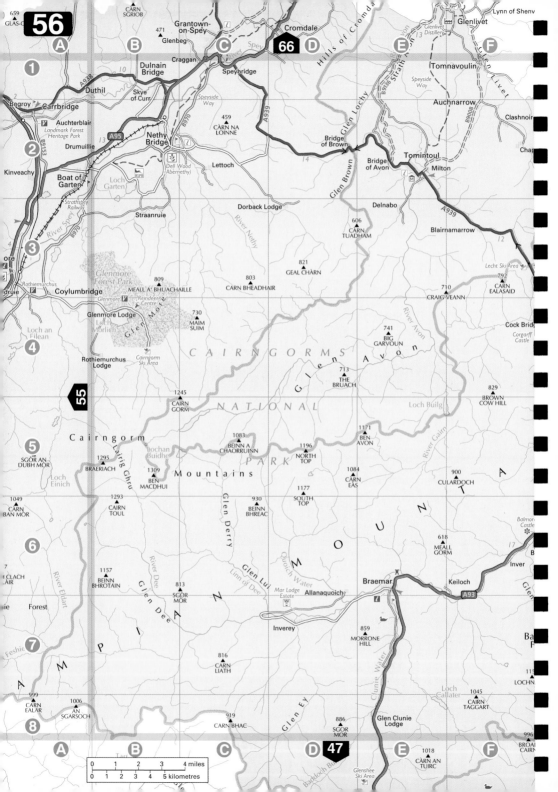

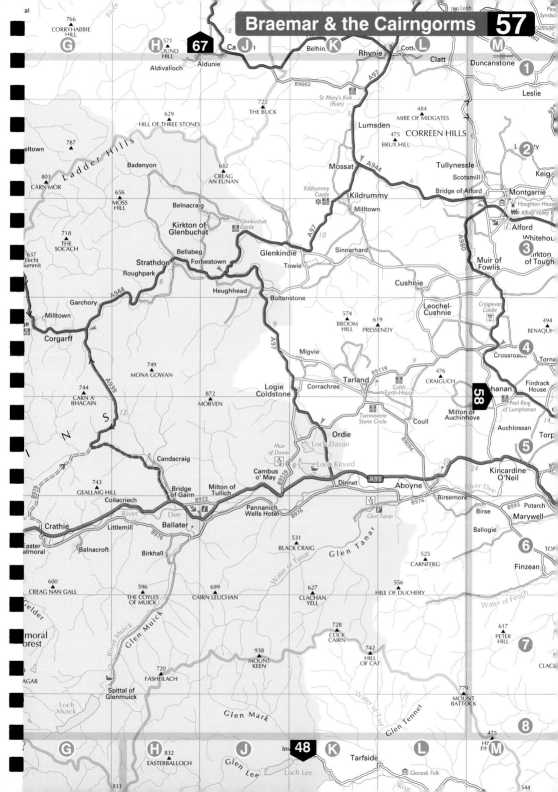

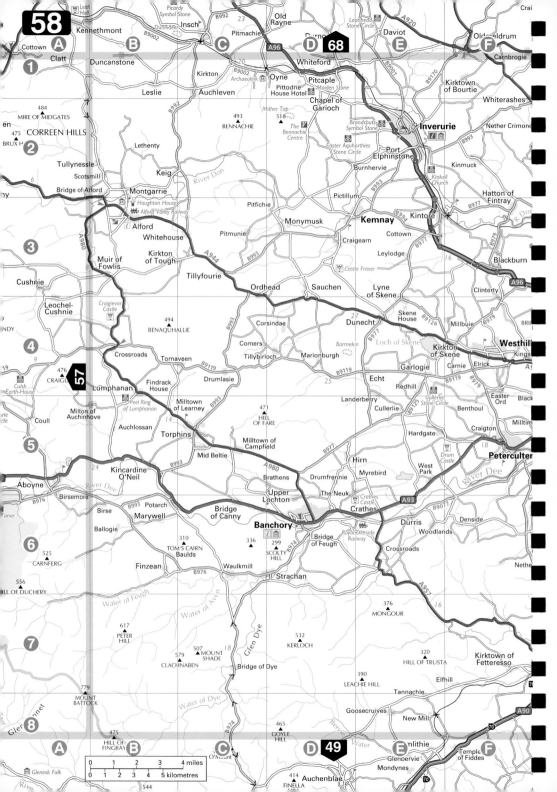

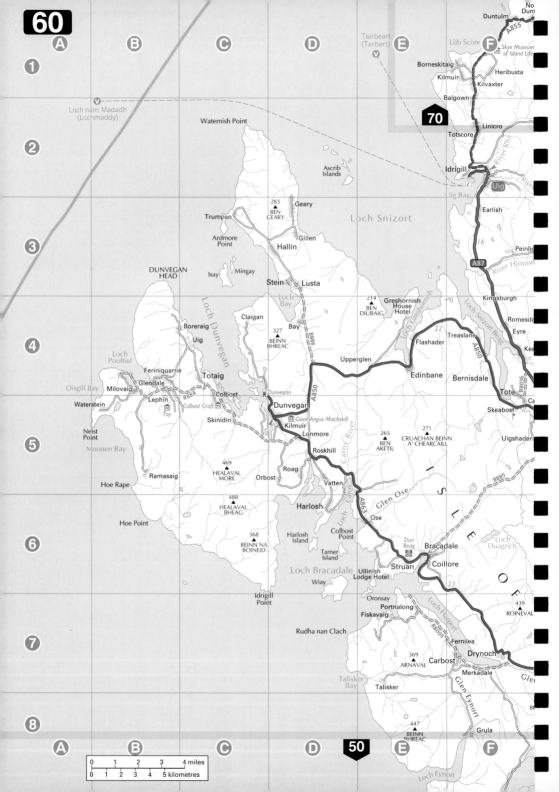

A   B   C   D   E   F

1

No Dun
Duntulm
A855
Lûb Score
Skye Museum
of Island Life

Borneskitaig
Kilmuir
Heribusta
Kilvaxter
Balgown

Tairbeart
(Tarbert)
70

Loch nam Madadh
(Lochmaddy)

2

Waternish Point

Linicro
Totscore

Idrigill

Earlish

Uig Bay
Uig

Ascrib
Islands

Loch Snizort

A87

River Hinniso

3

283
BEN
GEARY
Geary

Trumpan

Gillen

Ardmore
Point

Hallin

16

Peinlic

DUNVEGAN
HEAD

Isay
Mingay

Stein
Lusta

Loch
Bay

Kingsburgh

Romesda
Eyre

Loch Dunvegan

Claigan

Bay

214
BEN
DIUBAIG

Greshornish
House
Hotel

Ken

4

Boreraig
Uig

327
BEINN
BHREAC

B886

Upperglen

22
Treaslane

Flashader

A850

Bernisdale

B8036

Loch Pooltiel

Feriniquarrie
Glendale

Totaig

Colbost

Dunvegan

Edinbane

Tote

Oisgill Bay
Milovaig

Lephin

B884

Colbost Croft

Skinidin

Dunvegan

Skeabost

Ca

Waterstein

Toy

Kilmuir

A850

Uigshader

Neist
Point

Giant Angus MacAskill

Lonmore

265
BEN
AKETIL

271
CRUACHAN BEINN
A' CHEARCAILL

5

Moonen Bay

Roskhill

Caroy River

I
S
L
E

469
HEALAVAL
MORE

Roag

Vatten

B885

Ramasaig

Orbost

Hoe Rape

A863

Glen Ose

488
HEALAVAL
BHEAG

Harlosh

Ose

Loch
Duagrich

Hoe Point

368
BEINN NA
BOINEID

Harlosh
Island

Colbost
Point

Dun
Beag

Bracadale

Coillore

O

6

Idrigill
Point

Tarner
Island

Ullinish
Lodge Hotel

Struan

23

Loch Bracadale

Wiay

Loch Harport

439
ROINEVAL

Oronsay
Portnalong
Fiskavaig

B8009

Fernilea

O
F

7

Rudha nan Clach

369
ARNAVAL

Carbost

Drynoch

Merkadale

Glen Eynort

Gle

Talisker
Bay

Talisker

447
BEINN
BHREAC

Grula

8

A   B   C   D   E   F

50

Loch Eynort

0 1 2 3   4 miles
0 1 2 3 4 5 kilometres

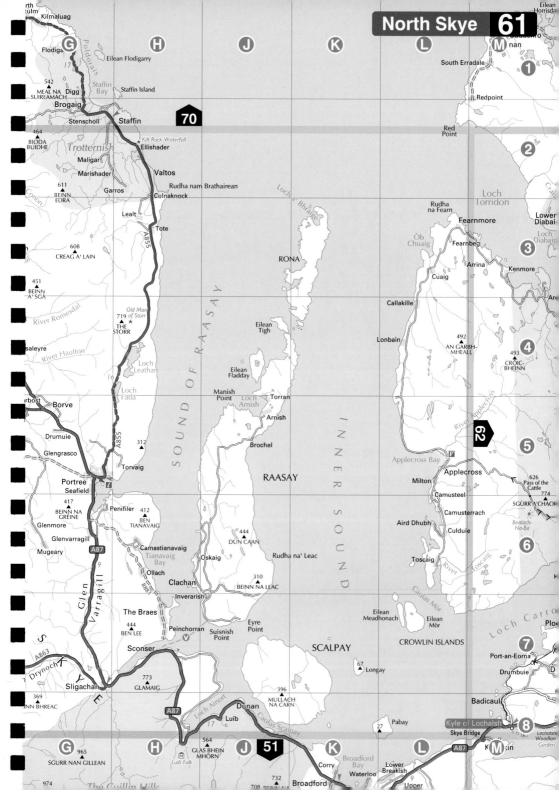

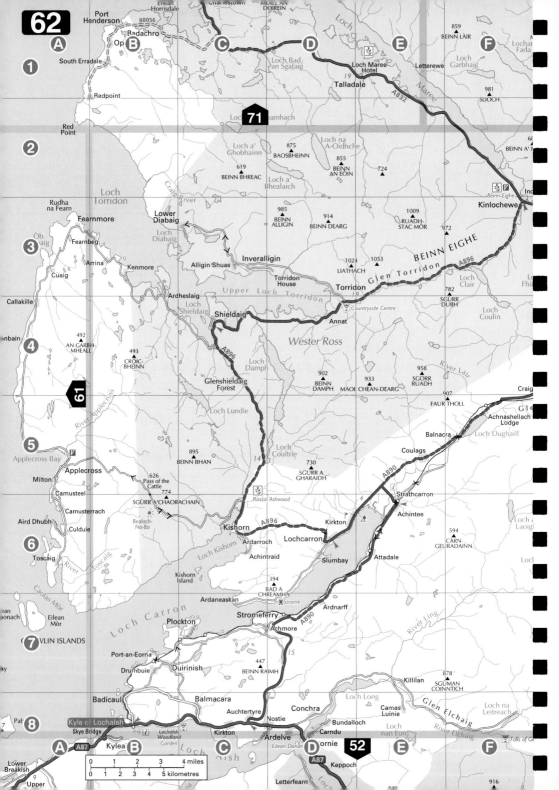

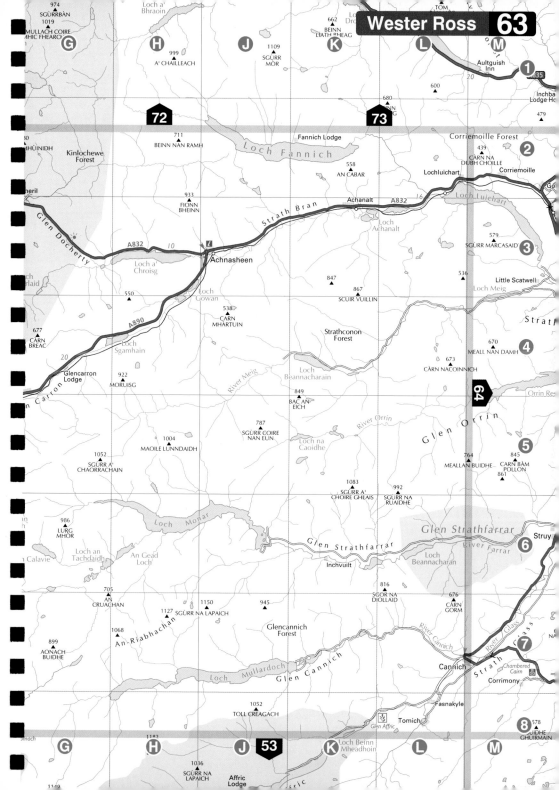

SGÙRRBÀN
1019

MULLACH COIRE
MHIC FHEARCHAIR
974

Loch a'
Bhraoin

G

H
999
A' CHAILLEACH

J
1109
SGÙRR
MÒR

TOM

BEINN
LIATH BHEAG
662

K

Loch Dro

L

M
Aultguish
Inn

1
A835

Inchba
Lodge Ho

600

680
NN
G

479

72

73

BEINN NAN RAMH
711

Fannich Lodge

Loch Fannich

Corriemoille Forest

2

MHÙINIDH
80

Kinlochewe
Forest

AN CABAR
558

CÀRN NA
DUBH CHOILLE
439

Lochluichart

Corriemoille

Go

heril

FIONN
BHEINN
933

Strath Bran

Achanalt

A832
16

Loch Luichart

Loch
Achanalt

SGÙRR MARCASAID
579

3

Glen Docherty

A832
10

Loch a'
Chroisg

Achnasheen

Little Scatwell

SCUIR VUILLIN
867

847

536

Loch Meig

Strath

550

Loch
Gowan

CÀRN
MHÀRTUIN
538

Strathconon
Forest

MEALL NAN DAMH
670

4

A890

CÀRN
BREAC
677

Loch
Sgamhain

20

Glencarron
Lodge

MORUISG
922

River Meig

Loch
Beannacharain

CÀRN NAÇOINNICH
673

Orrin Res

64

Carron

BAC AN
EICH
849

River Orrin

Glen Orrin

5

MAOILE LUNNDAIDH
1004

SGÙRR COIRE
NAN EUN
787

Loch na
Caoidhe

MEALLAN BUIDHE
764

CÀRN BÀN
POLLON
861
845

SGÙRR A'
CHAORRACHAIN
1052

SGÙRR A'
CHOIRE GHLAIS
1083

SGÙRR NA
RUAIDHE
992

LURG
MHÓR
986

Loch Monar

Glen Strathfarrar

Glen Strathfarrar

River Farrar

Struy

6

Calavie

Loch an
Tachdaidh

An Gead
Loch

Inchvuilt

Loch
Beannacharan

AN
CRUACHAN
705

SGÙRR NA LAPAICH
1127
1150

945

SGÙRR NA
DIOLLAID
816

CÀRN
GORM
676

River Cannich

River Glass

7

Strath

AONACH
BUIDHE
899

An-Riabhachan
1068

Glencannich
Forest

Cannich

Chambered
Cairn

Corrimony

Loch Mullardoch

Glen Cannich

Fasnakyle

TOLL CREAGACH
1052

Tomich

Glen Affric

M

GHUIRMAIN
578

8

1182

G

SGÙRR NA
LAPAICH
1036

H

Affric
Lodge

J **53**

Loch Beinn
Mheadhoin

K

L

M

1149

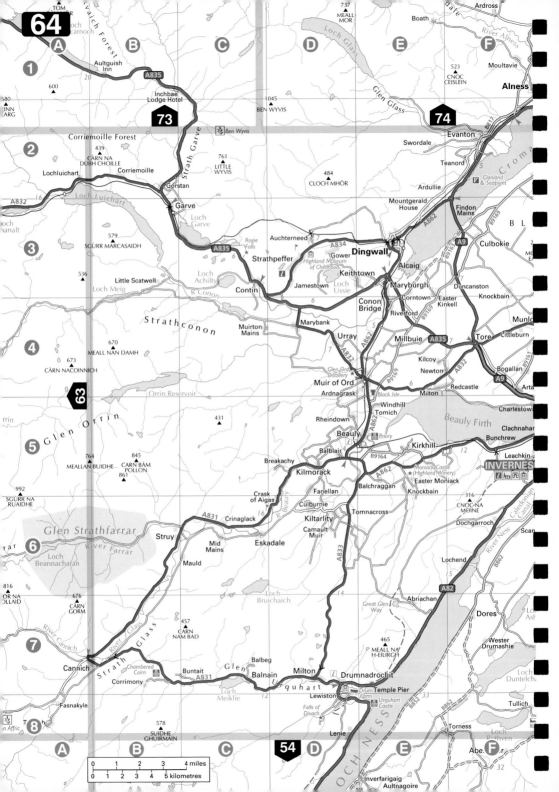

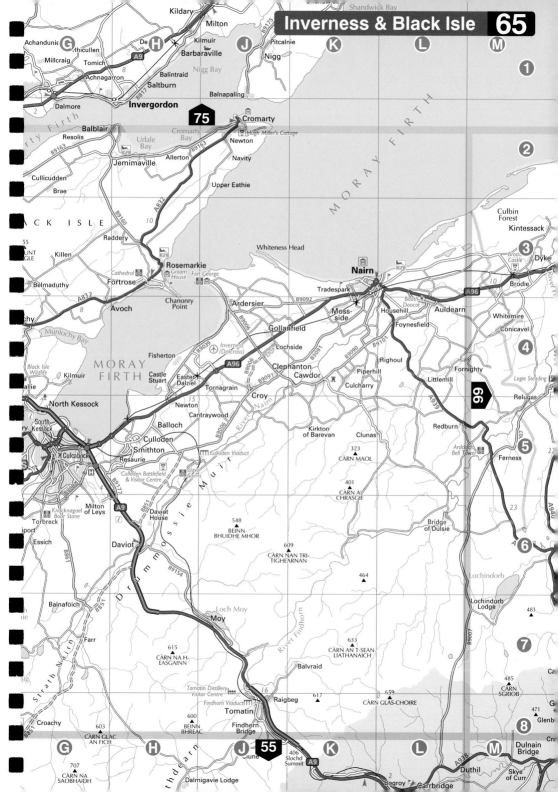

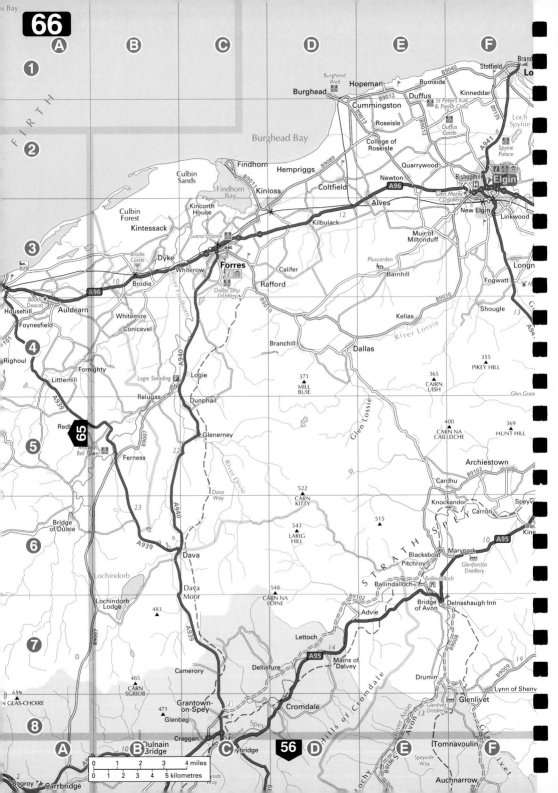

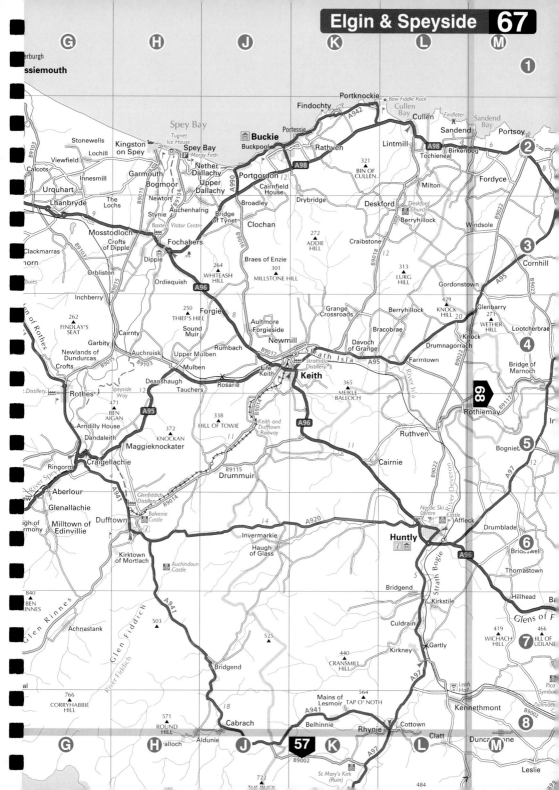

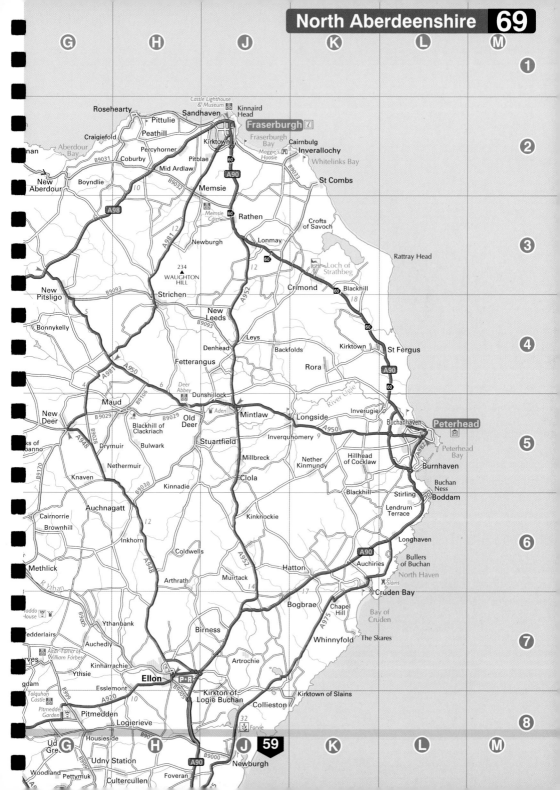

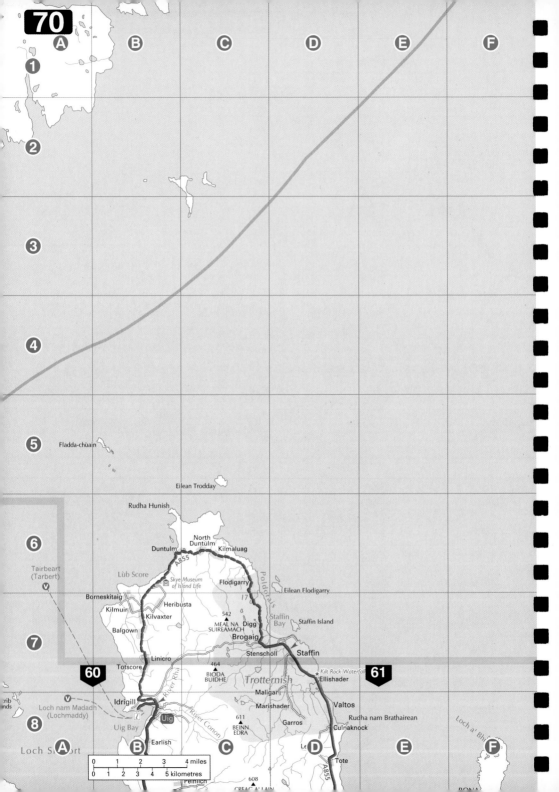

70

60
61

Fladda-chùain

Eilean Trodday

Rudha Hunish

North
Duntulm

Duntulm
Kilmaluag

A855

Lùb Score

Skye Museum
of Island Life

Flodigarry

Eilean Flodigarry

Polltorais

Borneskitaig

Heribusta

Kilmuir

Kilvaxter

Balgown

542
MEAL NA
SUIREAMACH

Digg

Staffin
Bay

Staffin Island

Brogaig

Linicro

Stenscholl

Staffin

Totscore

464
BIODA
BUIDHE

River Rha

Trotternish

Kilt Rock Waterfall

Ellishader

Tairbeart
(Tarbert)

Idrigill

Uig

Uig Bay

River Conon

Maligar

Marishader

611
BEINN
EDRA

Garros

Valtos

Rudha nam Brathairean

Culnaknock

Loch a' Bhi

Loch nam Madadh
(Lochmaddy)

Earlish

Le

Tote

A855

Loch S ort

Peinlich

608
CREAG A'LAIN

BONA

0   1   2   3   4 miles
0 1 2 3 4 5 kilometres

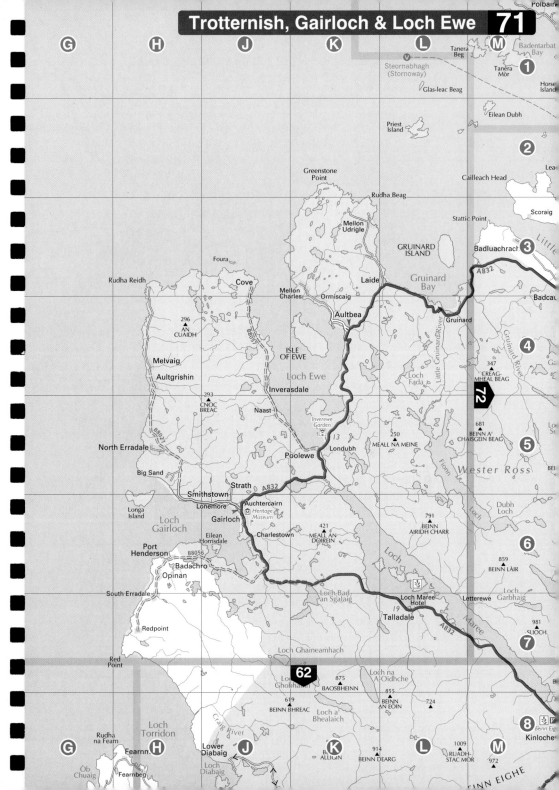

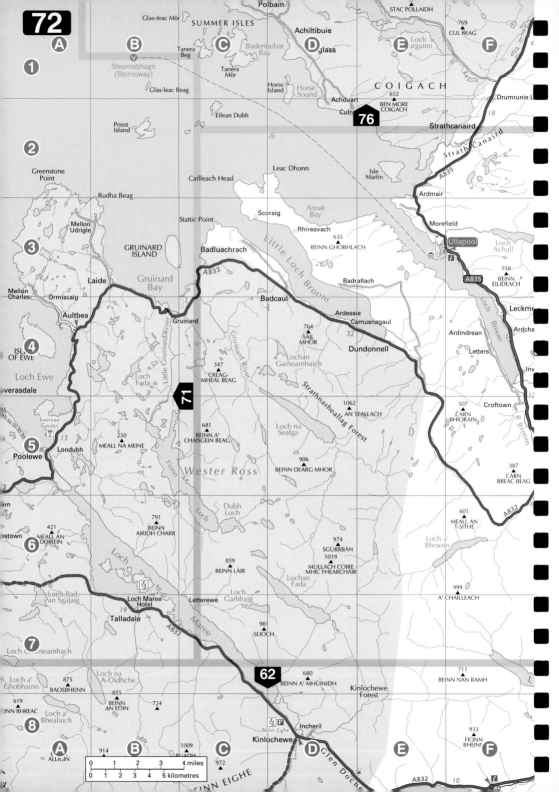

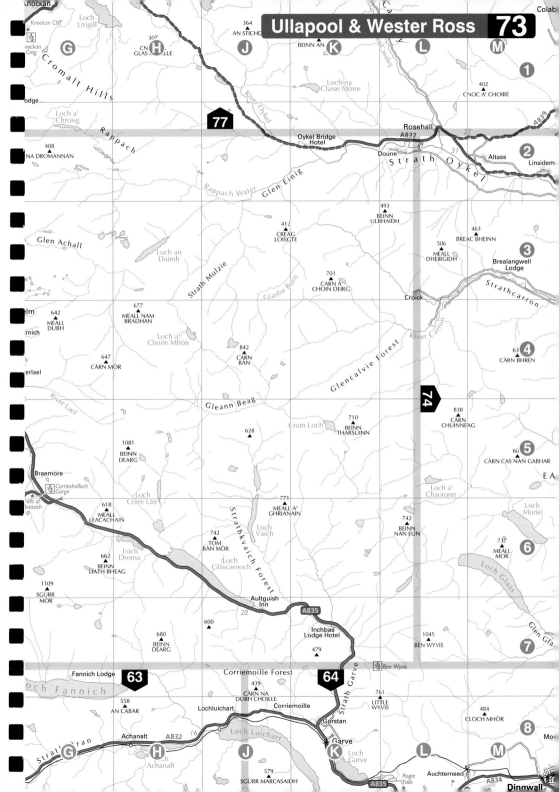

Colab

Knockan

Knockan Cliff

Loch Urigill

G

nockan Crag

307 **H** CN GLAS CNAILLE

364 **J** AN STICHD

BEINN AN **K**

L

M

1

Cromalt Hills

odge

Loch a' Chroisg

Rappach

Loch na Claise Moire

402 CNOC A' CHOIRE

A839

77

River Oykel

Rosehall

A837

27

2

NA DROMANNAN 408

Rappach Water

Glen Einig

Oykel Bridge Hotel

Doune

Strath Oykel

31

Altass

Linsidem

Glen Achall

Loch an Daimh

Strath Mulzie

Glasha Burn

412 CREAG LOISGTE

701 CARN A' CHOIN DEIRG

493 BEINN ULBHAIDH

506 MEALL DHEIRGIDH

463 BREAC BHEINN

3

Brealangwell Lodge

Strathcarron

Croick

River Carron

elm

642 MEALL DUBH

rnich

677 MEALL NAM BRADHAN

Loch a' Choire Mhòir

842 CARN BAN

63 CÀRN BHREN **4**

erlael

647 CÀRN MÓR

Glencalvie Forest

River Lael

Gleann Beag

Crom Loch

628

710 BEINN THARSUINN

838 CARN CHUINNEAG

74

5

66 CÀRN CAS NAN GABHAR

1081 BEINN DEARG

771 MEALL A' GHRIANAIN

Loch a' Chaorunn

E A

Braemore

Corrieshalloch Gorge

Falls of leasach

Loch Coire Làir

618 MEALL LEACACHAIN

Strathvaich Forest

Loch Vaich

742 BEINN NAN EUN

Loch Morie

737 MEALL MÓR **6**

662 BEINN LIATH BHEAG

Loch Droma

742 TOM BÀN MÓR

Loch Glascarnoch

1109 SGÙRR MÓR

Loch Glass

Glen Gla

1045 BEN WYVIS

7

680 BEINN DEARG

600

Aultguish Inn

20

A835

Inchbae Lodge Hotel

479

Ben Wyvis

Fannich Lodge **63**

Corriemoille Forest

64

Strath Garve

761 LITTLE WYVIS

484 CLOCH MHÒR

och Fannich

558 AN CABAR

439 CÀRN NA DUBH CHOILLE

Lochluichart

Corriemoille

8

Mo

Strath ran **G**

Achanalt

A832

16

Loch Luichart

H

Loch Achanalt

J

Gòrstan

Garve **K**

Loch Garve

L

Auchterneed

M

A834

Dingwall

579 SGÙRR MARCASAIDH

Rogie Falls

A835

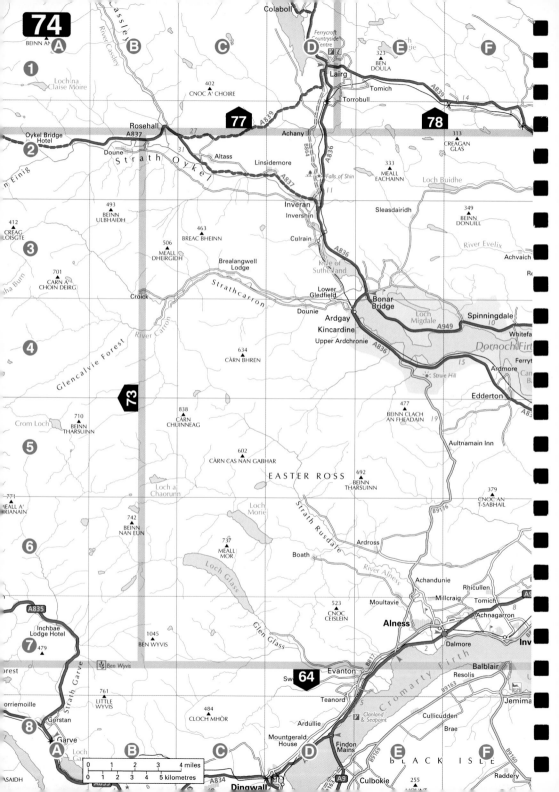

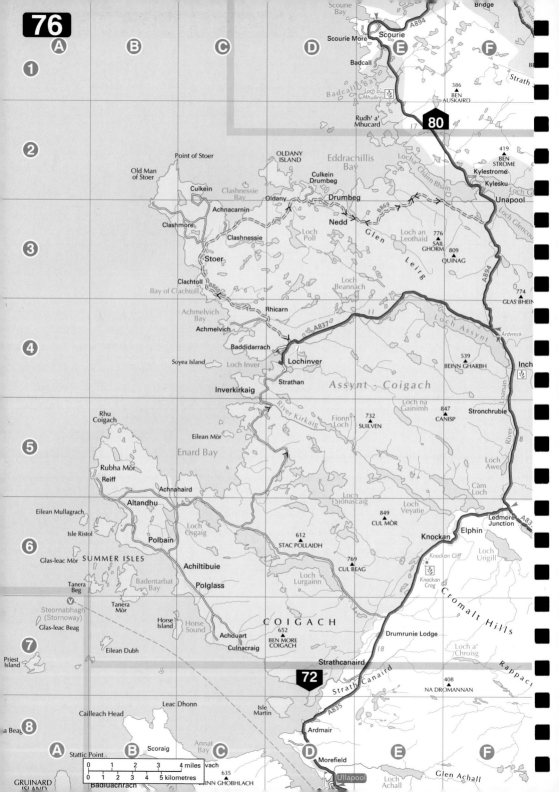

A B C D E F

1

2

3

4

5

6

7

8

Scourie Bay
Bridge

Scourie More Scourie
Badcall
Badcall Bay
Loch a' Mhuilinn
Rudh' a' Mhucard

386 ▲ BEN AUSKAIRD
Strath

A894

80

OLDANY ISLAND
Eddrachillis Bay
Lochan Charn Bhain
419 ▲ BEN STROME
Kylestrome
Kylesku
Unapool
Loch Glencoul
Loch Glen...

Point of Stoer
Old Man of Stoer
Culkein
Clashnessie Bay
Achnacarnin
Clashmore
Clashnessie
Oldany
Culkein Drumbeg
Drumbeg
Nedd
B869
Glen Leirg
Loch an Leothaid
776 ▲ SAIL GHORM
809 ▲ QUINAG
774 ▲ GLAS BHEIN

Stoer
Clachtoll
Bay of Clachtoll
Loch Poll
Loch Beannach

Rhicarn
A837
Achmelvich Bay
Achmelvich
Baddidarrach
Soyea Island
Loch Inver
Lochinver
Strathan

Loch Assynt
Ardvreck
539 ▲ BEINN GHARBH
Inch

Inverkirkaig
River Kirkaig
Fionn Loch
732 ▲ SUILVEN
Loch na Gainimh
847 ▲ CANISP
Stronchrubie

Assynt - Coigach

Rhu Coigach
Eilean Mòr
Enard Bay
River
Loch Awe

8

Rubha Mòr
Reiff
Achnahaird
Altandhu
Eilean Mullagrach
Isle Ristol
Polbain

Loch Osgaig
Loch Sionascaig
849 ▲ CUL MÒR
Loch Veyatie
Loch Awe
Càm Loch
Ledmore Junction
A83

612 ▲ STAC POLLAIDH
Knockan
Elphin
Knockan Cliff
Loch Urigill

Glas-leac Mòr
SUMMER ISLES
Achiltibuie
Polglass
769 ▲ CUL BEAG
Loch Lurgainn
Knockan Crag
Cromalt Hills
Rappac...

Tanera Beg
Badentarbat Bay
Steornabhagh (Stornoway)
Glas-leac Beag
Tanera Mòr
Horse Island
Horse Sound
Achduart
652 ▲ BEN MORE COIGACH
COIGACH

Priest Island
Eilean Dubh
Culnacraig
Drumrunie Lodge
Strathcanaird
72
Strath Canaird
18
408 ▲ NA DROMANNAN
Loch a' Chroisg

Cailleach Head
Leac Dhonn
Isle Martin
Ardmair
A835

...a Beag
Stattic Point
Scoraig
Annat Bay
Morefield
Ullapool
Loch Achall
Glen Achall
Rappac...

GRUINARD ISLAND
Badluachrach
...vach
635 ▲ BEINN GHOBHLACH

0 1 2 3 4 miles
0 1 2 3 4 5 kilometres

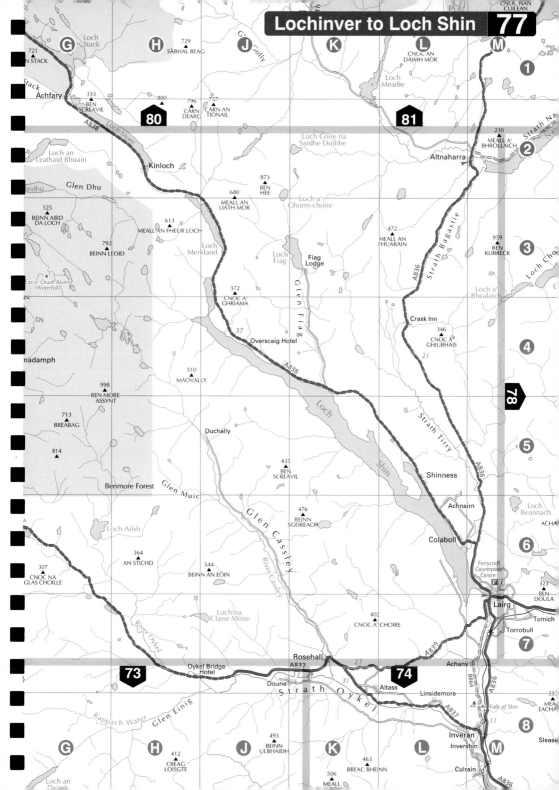

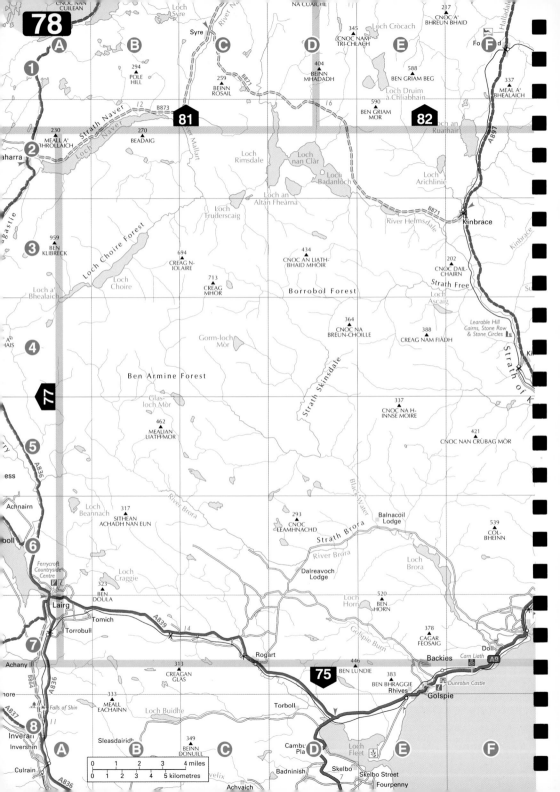

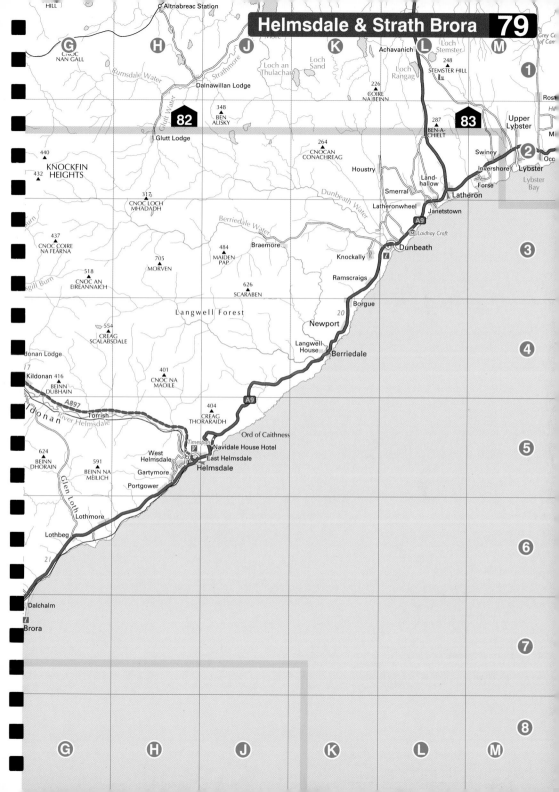

HILL
Altnabreac Station

G **H** **J** More **K** Achavanich **L** Loch Stemster **M**

CNOC NAN GALL

Loch an Thulachan

Loch Sand

Loch Rangag

248 STEMSTER HILL

Rost

1

Rumsdale Water

Strathmore

Dalnawillan Lodge

226 COIRE NA BEINN

287 BEN-A-CHIELT

Upper Lybster

Hi

82 348 BEN ALISKY **83**

Glutt Water

Glutt Lodge

264 CNOC AN CONACHREAG

Swiney

Invershore Lybster

Lybster Bay

2 Occ M

440

KNOCKFIN HEIGHTS

432

Houstry

Smerral Land-hallow Forse

317 CNOC LOCH MHADADH

Dunbeath Water

Latheronwheel Latheron

Janetstown

A9

3

437 CNOC COIRE NA FEARNA

Berriedale Water

Braemore

Laidhay Croft

Smerral

Dunbeath

Knockally

705 MORVEN

484 MAIDEN PAP

Ramscraigs

Dunbeath Burn

518 CNOC AN EIREANNAICH

626 SCARABEN

Borgue

4

Langwell Forest

20

Newport

554 CREAG SCALABSDALE

Langwell House Berriedale

onan Lodge

Kildonan 416 BEINN DUBHAIN

401 CNOC NA MAOILE

A9

5

A897

River Helmsdale

Torrish

404 CREAG THORARAIDH

Ord of Caithness

Idonan

Timespan

Navidale House Hotel

624 BEINN DHORAIN

591 BEINN NA MEILICH

West Helmsdale East Helmsdale

Helmsdale

Gartymore

6

Glen Loth

Portgower

Lothmore

Lothbeg

21

7

Dalchalm

Brora

8

G **H** **J** **K** **L** **M**

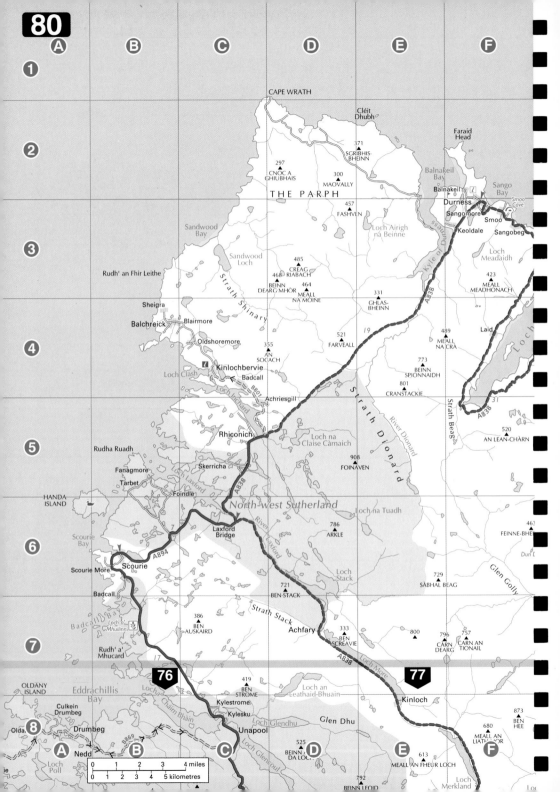

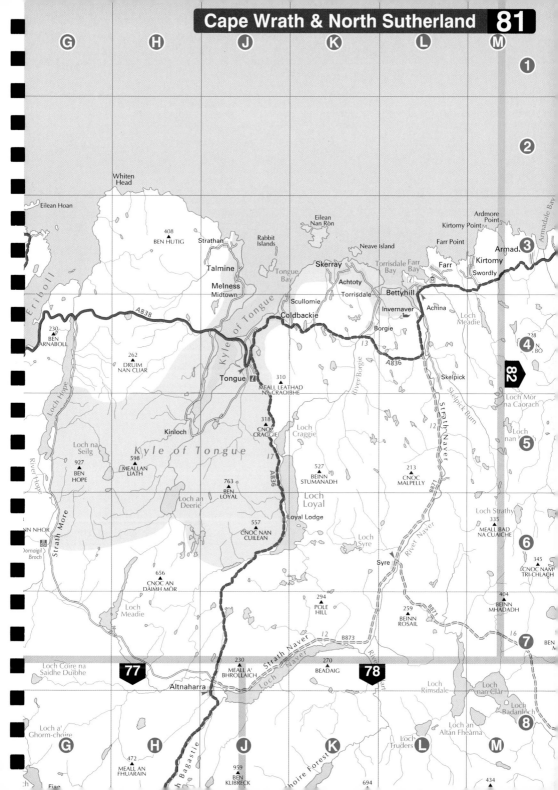

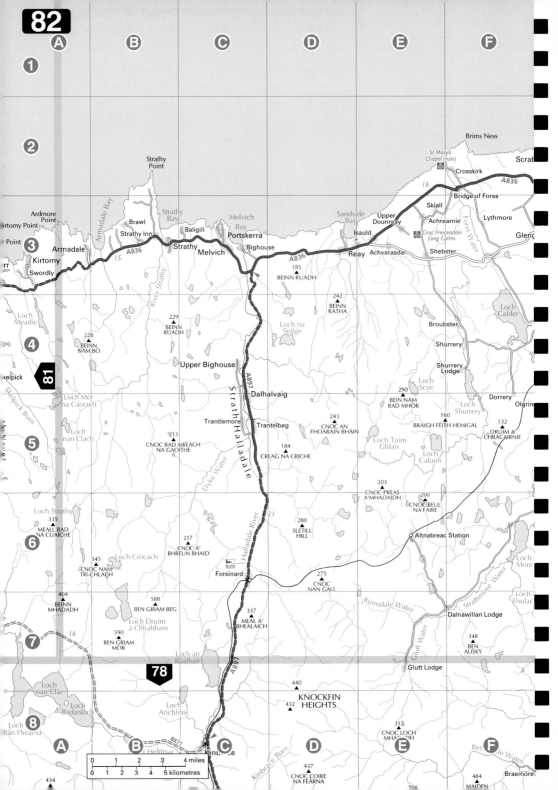

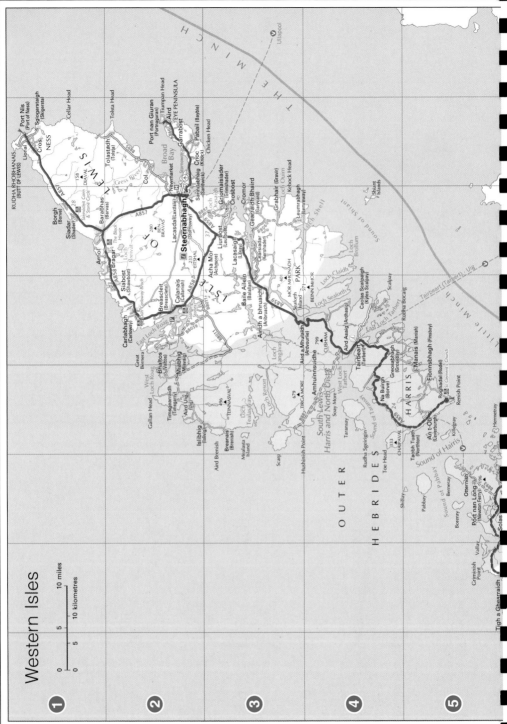

Western Isles

Ullapool

THE MINCH

Tarbeart (Tarbert), Uig

Little Minch

Shant Islands

Loch Seaforth

Loch Shell

Loch Bhrollum

Loch Ourn

Kebock Head

Grabhair (Grawir)
Leumrabhagh (Lemreway)
Gearraidh Bhaird (Garryvard)
Cromor
Crosbost
Griomaisiader (Grimshader)
Sanndabhaig (Sandwick)
Newmarket
Steòrnabhagh
Stornoway
Broad Bay
Tolastadh (Tolsta)
Tolsta Head
Cellar Head
Sgiogarstaigh (Skigersta)
Port Nis (Port of Ness)
RUDHA RHOBHANAIS (BUTT OF LEWIS)
Lional
Cros
NESS
Tumpan Head
Aird
EYE PENINSULA
Port nan Giuran (Portnaguran)
Garrabost
Pabail (Bayble)
Chicken Head
Cnoc (Knock)

Diabal
Muirneag
Cross River
Col

LEWIS

Borgh (Borve)
Barabhas (Barvas)
Siabost (Shawbost)
Arnol
Bragar
Siadar (Shader)
Calanais (Callanish)
Breascleit (Breasclete)
Carlabhagh (Carloway)
The Black House
Callanish Cairn & Stone Circle
Brèinval
BEN BRAVAS
EITSEAL
Lacasdail (Laxdale)
Acha Mòr (Achmore)
Lacasaigh (Laxay)
Liurbost (Leurbost)
Baile Ailein (Balallan)
Airidh a bhruaich (Arivruaich)
Aird a Mhulaidh (Ardvourlie)
Gearsiadar (Kershader)
MÒR MHÒNADH
Seaforth Island
Caolas Scalpaigh (Kyles Scalpay)
Scalpay
Eilean Chaluim Chille
Col
A857
A858
A859
B8011
B8059
B895

PARK

Great Bernera
Bhaltos (Valtos)
Miabhig (Miavaig)
Gallan Head
West Loch Roag
East Loch Roag
Timsgearraidh (Timsgarry)
Aird Uig
Islibhig (Islivig)
Breanais (Brenish)
Mealasta Island
Scarp
Aird Brenish
Hushinish Point
Rudha Sgeotairh
Loch Reasort
Loch Langavat
East Loch Roag
TEINNASVAL
TEALASVAL
TIRGA MORE
Soay More
Taransay
Toe Head
Taebh Tuath (Northton)
CHAPAVAL
Shillay
Pabbay
Boreray
Berneray
Sound of Harris
St Clement's Church
Rodel

SOUTH LEWIS
Harris and North Uist

HARRIS
Tairbeart (Tarbert)
Aird Asaig (Ardhasig)
Ceann a Bhaigh
Caolas an Scarp
Greosabhagh (Grosebay)
Na Buirgh (Borve)
An t-Ob (Leverburgh)
Fionnsbhagh (Finsbay)
Manais (Manish)
Ròghadal (Rodel)
Renish Point
Killegray
Ensay

OUTER HEBRIDES

Tigh a Ghearraidh
Griminish Point
Vallay
Otternish
Pòrt nan Long (Newton Ferry)
Solas
Sòlas

0 5 10 miles
0 5 10 kilometres

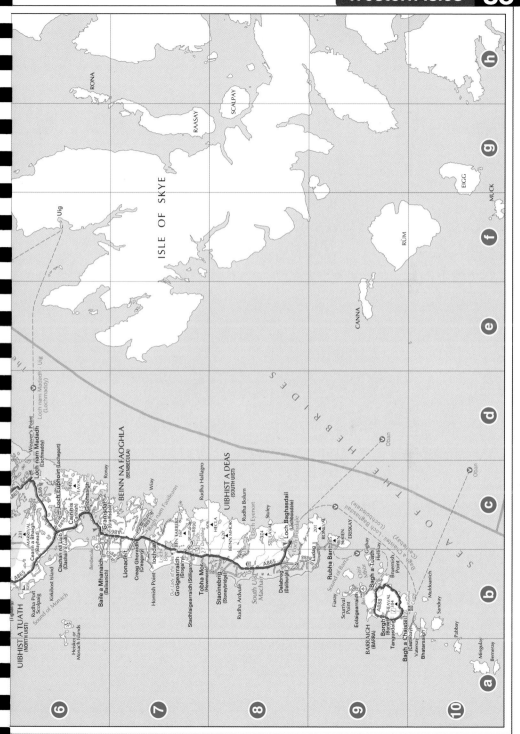

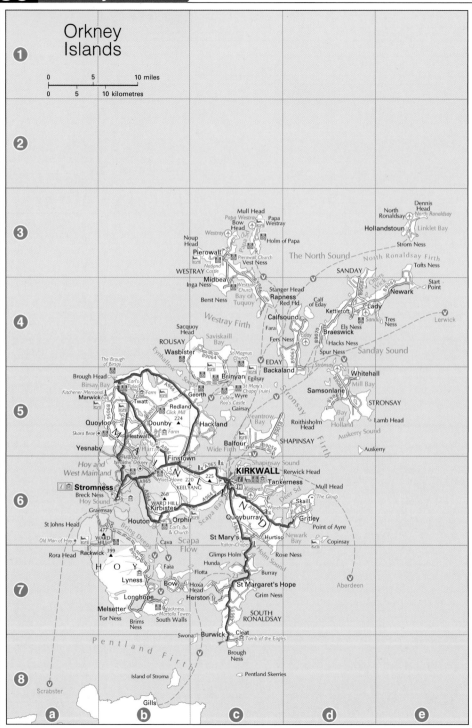

Orkney
Islands

0   5   10 miles
0   5   10 kilometres

Mull Head
Papa Westray   Papa
Bow   Westray
Noup   Head
Head   Westray
Holm of Papa
Pierowall   North
Vest Ness   Ronaldsay   Dennis
Pierowall Church   Hollandstoun   Head
Notland   North Ronaldsay
WESTRAY   Castle   The North Sound   Linklet Bay
Midbea   Westside   North Ronaldsay Firth
Inga Ness   Church   Strom Ness
SANDAY
Berst Ness   Bay of   Stanger Head   Tofts Ness
Tuquoy   Rapness   Els   Start
Red Hd.   Calf   Point
Calfsound   of Eday   Kettletoft   Lady   Sanday   Tres   Start
Sacquoy   Fara   Newark   Ness   Point
Head   Saviskaill   Els Ness
Bay   Fers Ness   Braeswick   Lerwick
ROUSAY   St Magnus   Hacks Ness
Wasbister   Church   EDAY   Spur Ness   Sanday Sound
The Brough   B9064   Backaland
of Birsay   Egilsay   Stronsay   Whitehall
Brough Head   Earl's   Brinyan   St Mary's   Mill Bay
Birsay Bay   Palace   Chapel (ruin)   Samsonlane
Kitchener Memorial   Georth   Wyre   STRONSAY
Marwick   Twatt   Cubbie   Roo's Castle   Gairsay   Veantrow   Bay of
Redland   Bay   Roithisholm   Holland
Quoyloo   Click Mill   Hackland   Head   Lamb Head
224   Auskerry Sound
Skara Brae   Dounby   Farm   Auskerry
Hestwall   SHAPINSAY
Yesnaby   Heart of   Finstown   Balfour   Shapinsay Sound
Neolithic Orkney   Wide Firth
Hoy and   A986   B9059   Auskerry
West Mainland   B965   KIRKWALL   Rerwick Head
Stromness   Moss Howe 220   225   Tankerness   Mull Head
Breck Ness   KEELYANG   Deer Sd.   The Gloup
Hoy Sound   WARD HILL   A965   Minehowe   Skaill
Graemsay   268   Kirbister   Gritley
St Johns Head   Houton   Orphir   Quoyburray   Point of Ayre
447   Earl's Bu   A960   Newark   Copinsay
Old Man of Hoy   WARD   & Church   St Mary's   Hurtiso   Bay
HILL   Cava   Scapa   Rose Ness
Rora Head   Rackwick   399   Flow   Glimps Holm   Burray
H O Y   Fata   Hunda   St Margaret's Hope   Aberdeen
Lyness   Flotta   Burray   Grim Ness
Longhope   Bow   Hoxa   SOUTH
Melsetter   Head   Herston   RONALDSAY
Tor Ness   Hackness   South Walls   Cleat   Tomb of the Eagles
Brims   Martello Tower   Burwick
Ness   Swona   Brough
Pentland Firth   Ness

Island of Stroma   Pentland Skerries

Scrabster   Gills

a   b   c   d   e

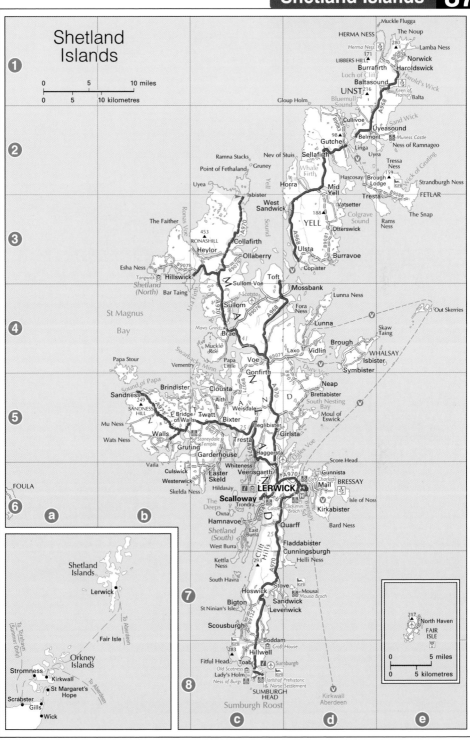

Mileage chart

The mileage chart shows distances in miles between two towns along AA-recommended routes. Using motorways and other main roads this is normally the fastest route, though not necessarily the shortest.

The journey times, shown in hours and minutes, are average off-peak driving times along AA-recommended routes. These times should be used as a guide only and do not allow for unforeseen traffic delays, rest breaks or fuel stops.

For example, the 378 miles (608 km) journey between Glasgow and Norwich should take approximately 7 hours 28 minutes.

journey times

The chart is a triangular mileage and journey-time matrix with the following towns along the diagonal:

Aberdeen, Aberystwyth, Barnstaple, Birmingham, Brighton, Bristol, Cambridge, Cardiff, Carlisle, Carmarthen, Dorchester, Dover, Edinburgh, Exeter, Fort William, Glasgow, Gloucester, Guildford, Hereford, Holyhead, Hull, Inverness, Kendal, Leeds, Lincoln, Liverpool, Maidstone, Manchester, Middlesbrough, Newcastle, Northampton, Norwich, Nottingham, Oxford, Penzance, Perth, Peterborough, Plymouth, Portsmouth, Preston, Salisbury, Sheffield, Shrewsbury, Southampton, Stoke-on-Trent, Stranraer, Taunton, Wick, York, LONDON

distances in miles (one mile equals 1.6093 km)

Index to place names

This index lists places appearing in the main-map section of the atlas in alphabetical order. The reference before each name gives the atlas page number and grid reference of the square in which the place appears. The map shows counties and administrative areas, together with a list of the abbreviated name forms used in the index. The top places of tourist interest are indexed in **red**, motorway service areas in **blue** and airports in blue *italic*.

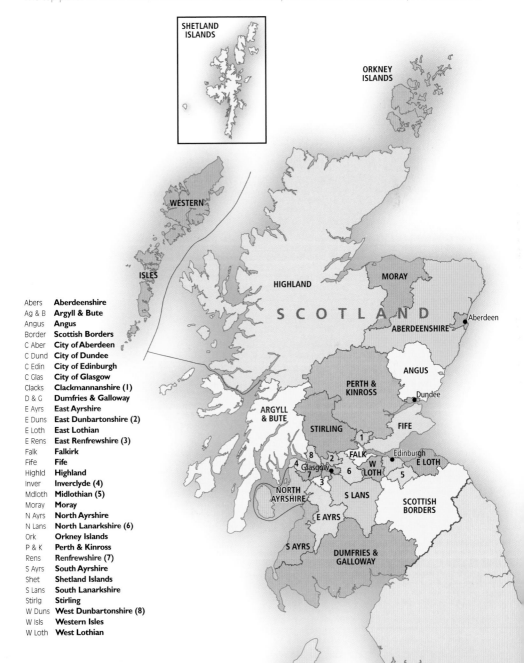

Abers	**Aberdeenshire**
Ag & B	**Argyll & Bute**
Angus	**Angus**
Border	**Scottish Borders**
C Aber	**City of Aberdeen**
C Dund	**City of Dundee**
C Edin	**City of Edinburgh**
C Glas	**City of Glasgow**
Clacks	**Clackmannanshire (1)**
D & G	**Dumfries & Galloway**
E Ayrs	**East Ayrshire**
E Duns	**East Dunbartonshire (2)**
E Loth	**East Lothian**
E Rens	**East Renfrewshire (3)**
Falk	**Falkirk**
Fife	**Fife**
Highld	**Highland**
Inver	**Inverclyde (4)**
Mdloth	**Midlothian (5)**
Moray	**Moray**
N Ayrs	**North Ayrshire**
N Lans	**North Lanarkshire (6)**
Ork	**Orkney Islands**
P & K	**Perth & Kinross**
Rens	**Renfrewshire (7)**
S Ayrs	**South Ayrshire**
Shet	**Shetland Islands**
S Lans	**South Lanarkshire**
Stirlg	**Stirling**
W Duns	**West Dunbartonshire (8)**
W Isls	**Western Isles**
W Loth	**West Lothian**

A

30 F6 **Abbey St Bathans** Border
19 J6 **Abbotrule** Border
38 B5 **Abbots Deuglie** P & K
54 F1 **Abererder** Highld
38 B4 **Aberargie** P & K
54 B5 **Aberchalder Lodge** Highld
68 C4 **Aberchirder** Abers
37 M4 **Aberdalgie** P & K
59 H4 **Aberdeen** C Aber
59 G3 *Aberdeen Airport* C Aber
29 G2 **Aberdour** Fife
46 D6 **Aberfeldy** P & K
36 C7 **Aberfoyle** Stirlg
30 B3 **Aberlady** E Loth
48 E5 **Aberlemno** Angus
67 G5 **Aberlour** Moray
38 C4 **Abernethy** P & K
38 D2 **Abernyte** P & K
37 K4 **Aberuthven** P & K
17 H5 **Abington** S Lans
17 H4 *Abington Services* S Lans
57 L5 **Aboyne** Abers
64 E7 **Abriachan** Highld
27 K3 **Abronhill** N Lans
40 F5 **Acha** Ag & B
24 D3 **Achahoish** Ag & B
47 H7 **Achalader** P & K
34 D1 **Achaleven** Ag & B
84 f3 **Acha Mor** W Isls
63 K3 **Achanalt** Highld
74 E6 **Achandunie** Highld
74 D2 **Achany** Highld
42 D3 **Acharacle** Highld
42 E6 **Acharn** Highld
46 B7 **Acharn** P & K
83 H6 **Achavanich** Highld
76 C7 **Achduart** Highld
80 D7 **Achfary** Highld
50 D4 **A'Chill** Highld
76 C6 **Achiltibuie** Highld
81 L4 **Achina** Highld
13 J6 **Achinhoan** Ag & B
62 E6 **Achintee** Highld
62 C6 **Achintraid** Highld
76 C4 **Achmelvich** Highld
62 D7 **Achmore** Highld
84 f3 **Achmore** W Isls
76 C3 **Achnacarnin** Highld
53 J7 **Achnacarry** Highld
51 J4 **Achnacloich** Highld
54 C2 **Achnaconeran** Highld
43 G7 **Achnacroish** Ag & B
41 L6 **Achnadrish House** Ag & B
37 J1 **Achnafauld** P & K
74 F7 **Achnagarron** Highld
41 L3 **Achnaha** Highld
76 B5 **Achnahaird** Highld
77 L6 **Achnairn** Highld
43 G4 **Achnalea** Highld
24 D2 **Achnamara** Ag & B
63 J3 **Achnasheen** Highld

62 F5 **Achnashellach Lodge** Highld
67 G7 **Achnastank** Moray
41 K3 **Achosnich** Highld
42 E6 **Achranich** Highld
82 E3 **Achreamie** Highld
44 B3 **Achriabhach** Highld
80 C5 **Achriesgill** Highld
81 K3 **Achtoty** Highld
74 F3 **Achvaich** Highld
82 E3 **Achvarasdal** Highld
83 L5 **Ackergill** Highld
28 D5 **Addiewell** W Loth
66 D7 **Advie** Highld
9 H4 **Ae** D & G
9 H5 **Ae Bridgend** D & G
68 B6 **Affleck** Abers
53 J2 **Affric Lodge** Highld
28 F5 **Ainville** W Loth
33 M7 **Aird** Ag & B
2 D3 **Aird** D & G
84 g2 **Aird** W Isls
84 e3 **Aird a Mhulaidh** W Isls
84 e4 **Aird Asaig** W Isls
61 L6 **Aird Dhubh** Highld
34 E2 **Airdeny** Ag & B
33 H2 **Aird of Kinloch** Ag & B
51 J4 **Aird of Sleat** Highld
27 K5 **Airdrie** N Lans
27 K5 **Airdriehill** N Lans
34 E2 **Airds Bay** Ag & B
8 B7 **Airds of Kells** D & G
84 d2 **Aird Uig** W Isls
84 e3 **Airidh a bhruaich** W Isls
4 D4 **Airieland** D & G
47 L6 **Airlie** Angus
38 A1 **Airntully** P & K
51 L4 **Airor** Highld
28 B2 **Airth** Falk
87 c5 **Aith** Shet
64 E3 **Alcaig** Highld
46 E4 **Aldclune** P & K
57 H1 **Aldivalloch** Moray
26 C1 **Aldochlay** Ag & B
67 H8 **Aldunie** Moray
26 D3 **Alexandria** W Duns
27 L6 **Allanbank** N Lans
31 H7 **Allanton** Border
27 L6 **Allanton** N Lans
27 K7 **Allanton** S Lans
65 H2 **Allerton** Highld
62 C3 **Alligin Shuas** Highld
37 J8 **Alloa** Clacks
15 J5 **Alloway** S Ayrs
44 C6 **Alltchaorunn** Highld
37 M3 **Almondbank** P & K
74 E7 **Alness** Highld
76 B6 **Altandhu** Highld
74 C2 **Altass** Highld
42 D8 **Altcreich** Ag & B
25 H4 **Altgaltraig** Ag & B
82 E6 **Altnabreac Station** Highld
34 B2 **Altnacraig** Ag & B
77 M2 **Altnaharra** Highld

36 B6 **Altskeith Hotel** Stirlg
37 J7 **Alva** Clacks
66 E3 **Alves** Moray
47 K6 **Alyth** P & K
84 d4 **Amhuinnsuidhe** W Isls
9 H5 **Amisfield Town** D & G
37 J1 **Amulree** P & K
43 G4 **Anaheilt** Highld
19 K4 **Ancrum** Border
75 H6 **Ankerville** Highld
5 L2 **Annan** D & G
9 J4 *Annandale Water Services* D & G
62 D4 **Annat** Highld
27 J4 **Annathill** N Lans
15 K5 **Annbank** S Ayrs
26 F5 **Anniesland** C Glas
39 J6 **Anstruther** Fife
84 d5 **An t-Ob** W Isls
3 M4 **Anwoth** D & G
43 J6 **Appin** Ag & B
61 L5 **Applecross** Highld
9 J5 **Applegarth Town** D & G
19 H6 **Appletreehall** Border
75 H6 **Arabella** Highld
48 F7 **Arbirlot** Angus
75 J5 **Arboll** Highld
49 G7 **Arbroath** Angus
49 K2 **Arbuthnott** Abers
26 D3 **Archencarroch** W Duns
66 F5 **Archiestown** Moray
69 J6 **Ardallie** Abers
34 F3 **Ardanaiseig Hotel** Ag & B
62 C7 **Ardaneaskan** Highld
62 C6 **Ardarroch** Highld
12 D1 **Ardbeg** Ag & B
25 J5 **Ardbeg** Ag & B
25 K2 **Ardbeg** Ag & B
72 F4 **Ardcharnich** Highld
32 E4 **Ardchiavaig** Ag & B
34 D5 **Ardchonnel** Ag & B
36 D5 **Ardchullarie More** Stirlg
35 J7 **Arddarroch** Ag & B
53 H7 **Ardechive** Highld
15 H2 **Ardeer** N Ayrs
62 D8 **Ardelve** Highld
26 C2 **Arden** Ag & B
34 B3 **Ardentallen** Ag & B
25 L2 **Ardentinny** Ag & B
25 H4 **Ardentraive** Ag & B
36 E1 **Ardeonaig** Stirlg
65 J4 **Ardersier** Highld
72 D4 **Ardessie** Highld
34 A6 **Ardfern** Ag & B
23 K4 **Ardfernal** Ag & B
74 D4 **Ardgay** Highld
43 K4 **Ardgour** Highld
25 L4 **Ardgowan** Inver
25 K4 **Ardhallow** Ag & B
84 e4 **Ardhasig** W Isls
62 B3 **Ardheslaig** Highld
72 F4 **Ardindrean** Highld
25 G5 **Ardlamont** Ag & B

47 L7 **Ardler** P & K
35 K4 **Ardlui** Ag & B
24 B2 **Ardlussa** Ag & B
43 L8 **Ardmaddy** Ag & B
72 E2 **Ardmair** Highld
25 J5 **Ardmaleish** Ag & B
24 B8 **Ardminish** Ag & B
42 E3 **Ardmolich** Highld
26 C3 **Ardmore** Ag & B
74 F4 **Ardmore** Highld
25 K3 **Ardnadam** Ag & B
64 E4 **Ardnagrask** Highld
62 D7 **Ardnarff** Highld
42 F4 **Ardnastang** Highld
35 G5 **Ardno** Ag & B
24 C6 **Ardpatrick** Ag & B
24 E2 **Ardrishaig** Ag & B
74 E6 **Ardross** Highld
15 G2 **Ardrossan** N Ayrs
42 B4 **Ardslignish** Highld
23 J7 **Ardtalla** Ag & B
42 C3 **Ardtoe** Highld
34 A5 **Arduaine** Ag & B
64 E2 **Ardullie** Highld
51 K5 **Ardvasar** Highld
36 D3 **Ardvorlich** P & K
84 e3 **Ardvourlie** W Isls
2 D5 **Ardwell** D & G
42 D3 **Arevegaig** Highld
35 J6 **Argyll Forest Park** Ag & B
84 e3 **Aribruach** W Isls
32 D3 **Aridhglas** Ag & B
40 F5 **Arileod** Ag & B
41 G5 **Arinagour** Ag & B
34 C3 **Ariogan** Ag & B
51 K7 **Arisaig** Highld
51 L7 **Arisaig House** Highld
10 C4 **Arkleton** D & G
51 K5 **Armadale** Highld
82 A3 **Armadale** Highld
28 C5 **Armadale** W Loth
40 F4 **Arnabost** Ag & B
39 H6 **Arncroach** Fife
67 G5 **Arndilly House** Moray
38 B5 **Arngask** P & K
52 C3 **Arnisdale** Highld
61 J5 **Arnish** Highld
29 K6 **Arniston** Mdloth
84 f1 **Arnol** W Isls
36 D7 **Arnprior** Stirlg
42 B7 **Aros** Ag & B
14 B3 **Arran** N Ayrs
62 B3 **Arrina** Highld
35 K6 **Arrochar** Ag & B
64 F4 **Artafallie** Highld
69 H6 **Arthrath** Abers
69 J7 **Artrochie** Abers
25 J5 **Ascog** Ag & B
37 G6 **Ashfield** Stirlg
27 K7 **Ashgill** S Lans
19 G5 **Ashkirk** Border
25 L3 **Ashton** Inver
24 F1 **Asknish** Ag & B
75 G3 **Astle** Highld
30 C3 **Athelstaneford** E Loth
62 E6 **Attadale** Highld
69 G7 **Auchedly** Abers
49 H1 **Auchenblae** Abers

27 L2 **Auchenbowie** Stirlg
4 D5 **Auchencairn** D & G
9 G5 **Auchencairn** D & G
14 D4 **Auchencairn** N Ayrs
31 H6 **Auchencrow** Border
29 H6 **Auchendinny** Mdloth
28 D7 **Auchengray** S Lans
67 J3 **Auchenhalrig** Moray
16 F2 **Auchenheath** S Lans
8 E3 **Auchenhessnane** D & G
25 G4 **Auchenlochan** Ag & B
26 C8 **Auchenmade** N Ayrs
2 F4 **Auchenmalg** D & G
26 C8 **Auchentiber** N Ayrs
36 C8 **Auchentroig** Stirlg
73 G5 **Auchindrean** Highld
68 C5 **Auchininna** Abers
16 B5 **Auchinleck** E Ayrs
27 H4 **Auchinloch** N Lans
27 J3 **Auchinstarry** N Lans
43 L2 **Auchintore** Highld
69 K6 **Auchiries** Abers
59 G6 **Auchlee** Abers
58 C1 **Auchleven** Abers
16 F3 **Auchlochan** S Lans
58 B5 **Auchlossan** Abers
36 B2 **Auchlyne** Stirlg
16 A4 **Auchmillan** E Ayrs
49 G7 **Auchmithie** Angus
38 C6 **Auchmuirbridge** Fife
48 D4 **Auchnacree** Angus
69 H6 **Auchnagatt** Abers
56 F2 **Auchnarrow** Moray
2 B3 **Auchnotteroch** D & G
67 H4 **Auchroisk** Moray
37 K5 **Auchterarder** P & K
54 B4 **Auchteraw** Highld
55 L2 **Auchterblair** Highld
71 J6 **Auchtercairn** Highld
38 C7 **Auchterderran** Fife
48 B8 **Auchterhouse** Angus
68 D6 **Auchterless** Abers
38 D5 **Auchtermuchty** Fife
64 D3 **Auchterneed** Highld
29 H1 **Auchtertool** Fife
62 C8 **Auchtertyre** Highld
36 C4 **Auchtubh** Stirlg
83 L3 **Auckengill** Highld
65 L4 **Auldearn** Highld
8 F5 **Auldgirth** D & G
27 H7 **Auldhouse** S Lans
52 E2 **Ault a' chruinn** Highld
71 K4 **Aultbea** Highld
71 H4 **Aultgrishin** Highld
73 J7 **Aultguish Inn** Highld
67 J4 **Aultmore** Moray

54 E2 **Aultnagoire** Highld
74 F5 **Aultnamain Inn** Highld
55 L3 **Aviemore** Highld
65 G4 **Avoch** Highld
28 B4 **Avonbridge** Falk
15 J5 **Ayr** S Ayrs
31 J6 **Ayton** Border

B

86 d4 **Backaland** Ork
69 J4 **Backfolds** Abers
75 H2 **Backies** Highld
51 K7 **Back of Keppoch** Highld
71 J6 **Badachro** Highld
80 B7 **Badcall** Highld
80 C4 **Badcall** Highld
72 D3 **Badcaul** Highld
76 D4 **Baddidarrach** Highld
28 F7 **Baddinsgill** Border
68 D6 **Badenscoth** Abers
57 H2 **Badenyon** Abers
62 B8 **Badicaul** Highld
17 K5 **Badlieu** Border
83 J5 **Badlipster** Highld
72 C3 **Badluachrach** Highld
75 G3 **Badninish** Highld
72 D3 **Badrallach** Highld
85 b9 **Bagh a Chaisteil** W Isls
85 b9 **Bagh a Tuath** W Isls
84 f3 **Baile Ailein** W Isls
85 b6 **Baile a Mhanaich** W Isls
32 D3 **Baile Mor** Ag & B
27 J5 **Baillieston** C Glas
68 B7 **Bainshole** Abers
38 F6 **Baintown** Fife
19 K6 **Bairnkine** Border
84 f3 **Balallan** W Isls
64 C7 **Balbeg** Highld
38 C2 **Balbeggie** P & K
64 D5 **Balblair** Highld
65 G2 **Balblair** Highld
4 E5 **Balcary** D & G
64 E5 **Balchraggan** Highld
80 B4 **Balchreick** Highld
39 K5 **Balcomie Links** Fife
39 G5 **Baldinnie** Fife
37 L4 **Baldinnies** P & K
39 G2 **Baldovie** C Dund
38 D2 **Baledgarno** P & K
40 C7 **Balemartine** Ag & B
29 G5 **Balerno** C Edin
38 D6 **Balfarg** Fife
48 E3 **Balfield** Angus
86 c5 **Balfour** Ork
26 F1 **Balfron** Stirlg
68 C6 **Balgaveny** Abers
48 E6 **Balgavies** Angus
37 L8 **Balgonar** Fife
2 D6 **Balgowan** D & G
54 F6 **Balgowan** Highld
70 B7 **Balgown** Highld
2 B3 **Balgracie** D & G
48 C8 **Balgray** Angus
17 H5 **Balgray** S Lans

47 L6 **Balhary** P & K
38 B1 **Balholmie** P & K
82 C3 **Baligill** Highld
47 L5 **Balintore** Angus
75 J6 **Balintore** Highld
75 G7 **Balintraid** Highld
85 b6 **Balivanich** W Isls
48 B7 **Balkeerie** Angus
25 H6 **Ballanlay** Ag & B
6 C5 **Ballantrae** S Ayrs
57 J6 **Ballater** Abers
75 G6 **Ballchraggan** Highld
30 B3 **Ballencrieff** E Loth
40 B6 **Ballevullin** Ag & B
13 L2 **Balliekine** N Ayrs
34 F7 **Balliemore** Ag & B
6 F4 **Balligmorrie** S Ayrs
24 F2 **Ballimore** Ag & B
36 C4 **Ballimore** Stirlg
66 E6 **Ballindalloch** Moray
38 D2 **Ballindean** P & K
38 C7 **Ballingry** Fife
46 F6 **Ballinluig** P & K
48 C5 **Ballinshoe** Angus
47 H5 **Ballintuim** P & K
65 H5 **Balloch** Highld
27 K4 **Balloch** N Lans
37 H4 **Balloch** P & K
7 G3 **Balloch** S Ayrs
26 D3 **Balloch** W Duns
58 B6 **Ballogie** Abers
41 K7 **Ballygown** Ag & B
23 G5 **Ballygrant** Ag & B
40 F5 **Ballyhaugh** Ag & B
8 B6 **Balmaclellan** D & G
4 C6 **Balmae** D & G
26 D1 **Balmaha** Stirlg
38 E5 **Balmalcolm** Fife
4 B5 **Balmangan** D & G
59 H2 **Balmedie** Abers
38 F3 **Balmerino** Fife
14 B3 **Balmichael** N Ayrs
57 G6 **Balmoral Castle Grounds** Abers
27 G4 **Balmore** E Duns
75 J5 **Balmuchy** Highld
48 F6 **Balmuir** Angus
29 G2 **Balmule** Fife
39 G4 **Balmullo** Fife
78 E6 **Balnacoil Lodge** Highld
62 F5 **Balnacra** Highld
57 G6 **Balnacroft** Abers
65 G7 **Balnafoich** Highld
46 E6 **Balnaguard** P & K
32 F1 **Balnahard** Ag & B
32 F7 **Balnahard** Ag & B
64 C7 **Balnain** Highld
80 F7 **Balnakeil** Highld
75 H7 **Balnapaling** Highld
37 L1 **Balquharn** P & K
36 C3 **Balquhidder** Stirlg
87 e1 **Baltasound** Shet
3 J3 **Baltersan** D & G
33 M4 **Balvicar** Ag & B
52 C3 **Balvraid** Highld
65 K7 **Balvraid** Highld
47 K6 **Bamff** P & K
43 L2 **Banavie** Highld
58 D6 **Banchory** Abers

59 G5 **Banchory-Devenick** Abers
38 C2 **Bandirran** P & K
68 D2 **Banff** Abers
5 H2 **Bankend** D & G
37 M1 **Bankfoot** P & K
16 C6 **Bankglen** E Ayrs
59 G4 **Bankhead** C Aber
17 J1 **Bankhead** S Lans
27 K3 **Banknock** Falk
9 L5 **Bankshill** D & G
27 L1 **Bannockburn** Stirlg
27 K3 **Banton** N Lans
84 f1 **Barabhas** W Isls
15 J3 **Barassie** S Ayrs
75 G6 **Barbaraville** Highld
15 K5 **Barbieston** S Ayrs
43 J7 **Barcaldine** Ag & B
27 G4 **Bardowie** E Duns
26 C4 **Bardrainney** Inver
3 G2 **Barfad** D & G
27 J5 **Bargeddie** N Lans
7 H6 **Bargrennan** D & G
27 H5 **Barlanark** C Glas
4 E4 **Barlochan** D & G
13 K1 **Barmollack** Ag & B
34 E8 **Barnacarry** Ag & B
4 E4 **Barnbarroch** D & G
2 D7 **Barncorkrie** D & G
49 G5 **Barnhead** Angus
39 H2 **Barnhill** C Dund
66 E3 **Barnhill** Moray
6 B7 **Barnhills** D & G
29 G4 **Barnton** C Edin
7 G4 **Barr** S Ayrs
85 b9 **Barra** W Isls
85 b9 *Barra Airport* W Isls
3 H5 **Barrachan** D & G
85 b9 **Barraigh** W Isls
40 B7 **Barrapoll** Ag & B
26 F6 **Barrhead** E Rens
6 F5 **Barrhill** S Ayrs
26 C7 **Barmill** N Ayrs
34 B3 **Barrnacarry Bay** Ag & B
83 J2 **Barrock** Highld
39 J1 **Barry** Angus
68 F7 **Barthol Chapel** Abers
84 f1 **Barvas** W Isls
19 K1 **Bassendean** Border
28 D5 **Bathgate** W Loth
28 C5 **Bathville** W Loth
48 D5 **Battledykes** Angus
58 B6 **Baulds** Abers
60 D4 **Bay** Highld
84 g2 **Bayble** W Isls
85 b6 **Bayhead** W Isls
26 F4 **Bearsden** E Duns
9 J2 **Beattock** D & G
64 E5 **Beauly** Highld
19 J5 **Bedrule** Border
4 F2 **Beeswing** D & G
85 c7 **Beinn Na Faoghla** W Isls
26 C7 **Beith** N Ayrs
30 E3 **Belhaven** E Loth
59 H2 **Belhelvie** Abers
67 K8 **Belhinnie** Abers
57 H3 **Bellabeg** Abers
34 A8 **Bellanoch** Ag & B
47 K4 **Bellaty** Angus

16 F3 **Bellfield** S Lans
17 J5 **Bellfield** S Lans
13 H2 **Belloch** Ag & B
13 H3 **Bellochantuy**
Ag & B
27 J6 **Bellshill** N Lans
27 L6 **Bellside** N Lans
28 E5 **Bellsquarry** W Loth
65 G3 **Belmaduthy** Highld
15 J5 **Belmont** S Ayrs
87 d2 **Belmont** Shet
57 J3 **Belnacraig** Abers
19 J4 **Belses** Border
85 c7 **Benbecula** W Isls
85 c6 *Benbecula Airport*
W Isls
8 C3 **Benbuie** D & G
43 H8 **Benderloch** Ag & B
49 K3 **Benholm** Abers
25 K2 **Benmore** Ag & B
14 C5 **Bennan** N Ayrs
44 B3 **Ben Nevis** Highld
15 J2 **Benslie** N Ayrs
58 F5 **Benthoul** C Aber
10 B4 **Bentpath** D & G
38 E2 **Benvie** Angus
51 L6 **Beoraidbeg** Highld
52 C2 **Bernera** Highld
60 F4 **Bernisdale** Highld
79 K4 **Berriedale** Highld
67 L3 **Berryhillock** Moray
67 L4 **Berryhillock** Moray
81 L3 **Bettyhill** Highld
84 d2 **Bhaltos** W Isls
85 b10 **Bhatarsaigh** W Isls
59 G5 **Bieldside** C Aber
3 H6 **Big Balcraig** D & G
8 B3 **Big Carlae** D & G
17 K2 **Biggar** S Lans
10 B6 **Bigholms** D & G
82 C3 **Bighouse** Highld
71 H5 **Big Sand** Highld
87 c7 **Bigton** Shet
83 K5 **Bilbster** Highld
29 H5 **Bilston** Mdloth
28 B4 **Binniehill** Falk
20 B2 **Birgham** Border
75 G3 **Birichin** Highld
67 L2 **Birkenbog** Abers
68 E5 **Birkenhills** Abers
57 H6 **Birkhall** Abers
38 F1 **Birkhill** Angus
18 B6 **Birkhill** D & G
47 G7 **Birnam** P & K
69 J7 **Birness** Abers
58 B6 **Birse** Abers
57 L5 **Birsemore** Abers
27 G4 **Bishopbriggs**
E Duns
66 F2 **Bishopmill** Moray
26 E4 **Bishopton** Rens
87 c5 **Bixter** Shet
31 H7 **Blackadder** Border
58 F3 **Blackburn** Abers
28 D5 **Blackburn** W Loth
16 C7 **Blackcraig** E Ayrs
34 D1 **Black Crofts** Ag & B
59 H3 **Blackdog** Abers
37 J5 **Blackford** P & K
29 G4 **Blackhall** C Edin
18 F2 **Blackhaugh** Border
69 K3 **Blackhill** Abers

69 K5 **Blackhill** Abers
69 H5 **Blackhill of**
Clackriach Abers
17 K7 **Blacklaw** D & G
47 J4 **Blacklunans** P & K
28 E3 **Blackness** Falk
28 B5 **Blackridge** W Loth
66 E6 **Blacksboat** Moray
5 J2 **Blackshaw** D & G
59 G4 **Blacktop** C Aber
14 A4 **Blackwaterfoot**
N Ayrs
8 F5 **Blackwood** D & G
16 F1 **Blackwood** S Lans
3 J4 **Bladnoch** D & G
43 K2 **Blaich** Highld
42 D3 **Blain** Highld
46 D4 **Blair Atholl** P & K
36 F7 **Blair Drummond**
Stirlg
47 J7 **Blairgowrie** P & K
28 D2 **Blairhall** Fife
37 K7 **Blairingone** P & K
37 H7 **Blairlogie** Stirlg
25 L2 **Blairmore** Ag & B
80 C4 **Blairmore** Highld
56 F3 **Blairnamarrow**
Moray
25 G4 **Blair's Ferry** Ag & B
26 F3 **Blanefield** Stirlg
27 J6 **Blantyre** S Lans
43 L3 **Blar a' Chaorainn**
54 F6 **Blargie** Highld
43 L3 **Blarmachfoldach**
Highld
8 B5 **Blawquhairn** D & G
39 G4 **Blebocraigs** Fife
30 B6 **Blegbie** E Loth
19 J4 **Bloomfield** Border
17 M1 **Blyth Bridge** Border
30 D7 **Blythe** Border
39 J5 **Boarhills** Fife
74 D6 **Boath** Highld
55 L2 **Boat of Garten**
Highld
69 L6 **Boddam** Abers
87 c7 **Boddam** Shet
64 F4 **Bogallan** Highld
69 J7 **Bogbrae** Abers
15 K3 **Bogend** S Ayrs
29 L4 **Boggs Holdings**
E Loth
29 H5 **Boghall** Mdloth
28 D5 **Boghall** W Loth
16 F2 **Boghead** S Lans
67 H2 **Bogmoor** Moray
49 G3 **Bogmuir** Abers
68 B5 **Bogniebrae** Abers
55 L2 **Bogroy** Highld
8 B6 **Bogue** D & G
53 L8 **Bohuntine** Highld
49 G6 **Bolshan** Angus
57 J3 **Boltenstone** Abers
30 B4 **Bolton** E Loth
74 E3 **Bonar Bridge**
Highld
34 E2 **Bonawe** Ag & B
19 J6 **Bonchester Bridge**
Border
28 D3 **Bo'ness** Falk
26 D3 **Bonhill** W Duns

19 K5 **Bonjedward** Border
27 L6 **Bonkle** N Lans
48 F7 **Bonnington** Angus
38 F6 **Bonnybank** Fife
27 L3 **Bonnybridge** Falk
69 G4 **Bonnykelly** Abers
29 J5 **Bonnyrigg** Mdloth
48 B8 **Bonnyton** Angus
9 M7 **Bonshaw Tower**
D & G
19 J1 **Boon** Border
9 L4 **Boreland** D & G
60 C4 **Boreraig** Highld
84 f1 **Borgh** W Isls
85 b9 **Borgh** W Isls
81 K4 **Borgie** Highld
4 B5 **Borgue** D & G
79 K4 **Borgue** Highld
70 B7 **Borneskitaig** Highld
4 A5 **Borness** D & G
28 D3 **Borrowstoun** Falk
18 F6 **Borthwickbrae**
Border
18 F6 **Borthwickshiels**
Border
61 G5 **Borve** Highld
84 d4 **Borve** W Isls
84 f1 **Borve** W Isls
85 b9 **Borve** W Isls
27 J6 **Bothwell** S Lans
27 J6 **Bothwell Services**
S Lans
38 F3 **Bottomcraig** Fife
41 G4 **Bousd** Ag & B
86 b7 **Bow** Ork
19 H4 **Bowden** Border
83 J3 **Bower** Highld
83 J3 **Bowermadden**
Highld
28 F1 **Bowershall** Fife
5 H2 **Bowhouse** D & G
19 G2 **Bowland** Border
26 E4 **Bowling** W Duns
22 F6 **Bowmore** Ag & B
38 E5 **Bow of Fife** Fife
48 E6 **Bowriefauld** Angus
68 C2 **Boyndie** Abers
69 G2 **Boyndlie** Abers
49 G6 **Boysack** Angus
83 K2 **Brabstermire**
Highld
60 E6 **Bracadale** Highld
27 K5 **Brackenhirst** N Lans
53 J8 **Brackletter** Highld
37 H5 **Braco** P & K
67 L4 **Bracobrae** Moray
51 L6 **Bracora** Highld
51 L6 **Bracorina** Highld
65 G2 **Brae** Highld
87 C4 **Brae** Shet
27 K3 **Braeface** Falk
49 H5 **Braehead** Angus
3 J4 **Braehead** D & G
28 C7 **Braehead** S Lans
56 E6 **Braemar** Abers
73 G5 **Braemore** Highld
79 J3 **Braemore** Highld
53 L6 **Brae Roy Lodge**
Highld
25 L4 **Braeside** Inver
47 L5 **Braes of Coul**
Angus

67 J3 **Braes of Enzie**
Moray
86 d4 **Braeswick** Ork
34 D6 **Braevallich** Ag & B
84 f2 **Bragar** W Isls
27 L8 **Braidwood** S Lans
42 B3 **Branault** Highld
66 D4 **Branchill** Moray
66 F1 **Branderburgh**
Moray
58 D5 **Brathens** Abers
82 B3 **Brawl** Highld
64 D5 **Breakachy** Highld
74 C3 **Brealangwell**
Lodge Highld
84 d3 **Breanais** W Isls
84 e2 **Breascleit** W Isls
84 e2 **Breasclete** W Isls
48 F4 **Brechin** Angus
8 E4 **Breckonside** D & G
28 C6 **Breich** W Loth
24 E2 **Brenfield** Ag & B
84 d3 **Brenish** W Isls
87 d6 **Bressay** Shet
87 d5 **Brettabister** Shet
68 B6 **Brideswell** Abers
67 L7 **Bridgend** Abers
23 G6 **Bridgend** Ag & B
48 E3 **Bridgend** Angus
17 L7 **Bridgend** D & G
38 F5 **Bridgend** Fife
67 J7 **Bridgend** Moray
38 B3 **Bridgend** P & K
28 E3 **Bridgend** W Loth
47 L5 **Bridgend of**
Lintrathen Angus
58 B2 **Bridge of Alford**
Abers
37 G7 **Bridge of Allan**
Stirlg
56 E2 **Bridge of Avon**
Moray
66 E7 **Bridge of Avon**
Moray
45 J6 **Bridge of Balgie**
P & K
47 J4 **Bridge of**
Brewlands Angus
56 D2 **Bridge of Brown**
Highld
47 J6 **Bridge of Cally**
P & K
58 C6 **Bridge of Canny**
Abers
47 K5 **Bridge of Craigisla**
Angus
4 C3 **Bridge of Dee**
D & G
59 H4 **Bridge of Don**
C Aber
65 L6 **Bridge of Dulsie**
Highld
58 C7 **Bridge of Dye**
Abers
38 B4 **Bridge of Earn**
P & K
45 H5 **Bridge of Ericht**
P & K
58 D6 **Bridge of Feugh**
Abers
82 F2 **Bridge of Forss**
Highld

57 H6 **Bridge of Gairn** Abers
45 H5 **Bridge of Gaur** P & K
68 B4 **Bridge of Marnoch** Abers
44 E7 **Bridge of Orchy** Ag & B
46 D4 **Bridge of Tilt** P & K
67 J3 **Bridge of Tynet** Moray
87 b5 **Bridge of Walls** Shet
26 D5 **Bridge of Weir** Rens
28 C3 **Brightons** Falk
36 C6 **Brig o'Turk** Stirlg
87 c5 **Brindister** Shet
86 c5 **Brinyan** Ork
26 C4 **Broadfield** Inver
51 K2 **Broadford** Highld
18 C7 **Broadgairhill** Border
31 H7 **Broadhaugh** Border
67 J3 **Broadley** Moray
61 J5 **Brochel** Highld
16 F2 **Brocketsbrae** S Lans
14 C3 **Brodick** N Ayrs
66 B3 **Brodie** Moray
70 C7 **Brogaig** Highld
26 D5 **Brookfield** Rens
78 F7 **Brora** Highld
82 F4 **Broubster** Highld
83 J2 **Brough** Highld
87 d4 **Brough** Shet
87 d2 **Brough Lodge** Shet
17 L3 **Broughton** Border
3 J6 **Broughton Mains** D & G
39 H2 **Broughty Ferry** C Dund
69 G6 **Brownhill** Abers
39 H4 **Brownhills** Fife
30 E3 **Broxburn** E Loth
28 E4 **Broxburn** W Loth
83 K7 **Bruan** Highld
46 C3 **Bruar** P & K
75 K4 **Brucefield** Highld
25 J6 **Bruchag** Ag & B
22 E6 **Bruichladdich** Ag & B
42 E3 **Brunery** Highld
38 E3 **Brunton** Fife
9 L7 **Brydekirk** D & G
50 F2 **Bualintur** Highld
18 E6 **Buccleuch** Border
26 E1 **Buchanan Smithy** Stirlg
69 L5 **Buchanhaven** Abers
37 J2 **Buchanty** P & K
36 F6 **Buchany** Stirlg
36 C8 **Buchlyvie** Stirlg
38 F7 **Buckhaven** Fife
67 J2 **Buckie** Moray
67 J2 **Buckpool** Moray
59 G4 **Bucksburn** C Aber
39 H2 **Buddon** Angus
69 H5 **Bulwark** Abers
51 K7 **Bunacaimb** Highld
53 J7 **Bunarkaig** Highld
64 F5 **Bunchrew** Highld

62 D8 **Bundalloch** Highld
32 E3 **Bunessan** Ag & B
23 H4 **Bunnahabhain** Ag & B
64 C7 **Buntait** Highld
41 J7 **Burg** Ag & B
66 D1 **Burghead** Moray
28 B6 **Burnbrae** N Lans
18 F6 **Burnfoot** Border
19 H6 **Burnfoot** Border
9 G4 **Burnfoot** D & G
10 C3 **Burnfoot** D & G
10 C4 **Burnfoot** D & G
37 K6 **Burnfoot** P & K
69 L5 **Burnhaven** Abers
8 E3 **Burnhead** D & G
58 D2 **Burnhervie** Abers
26 D7 **Burnhouse** N Ayrs
31 K6 **Burnmouth** Border
36 F6 **Burn of Cambus** Stirlg
48 C4 **Burnside** Angus
48 E6 **Burnside** Angus
38 B5 **Burnside** Fife
66 E1 **Burnside** Moray
28 E3 **Burnside** W Loth
39 G1 **Burnside of Duntrune** Angus
29 H2 **Burntisland** Fife
87 e1 **Burrafirth** Shet
87 d3 **Burravoe** Shet
47 K8 **Burrelton** P & K
86 c8 **Burwick** Ork
27 G6 **Busby** E Rens
49 J4 **Bush** Abers
25 H4 **Bute** Ag & B
31 G5 **Butterdean** Border
47 G7 **Butterstone** P & K

C

23 J5 **Cabrach** Ag & B
67 J8 **Cabrach** Moray
27 G4 **Cadder** E Duns
19 G3 **Caddonfoot** Border
38 D6 **Cadham** Fife
10 D2 **Caerlanrig** Border
85 c6 **Cairinis** W Isls
24 E1 **Cairnbaan** Ag & B
69 J2 **Cairnbulg** Abers
31 J5 **Cairncross** Border
26 C4 **Cairncurran** Inver
35 H5 **Cairndow** Ag & B
28 E2 **Cairneyhill** Fife
67 J3 **Cairnfield House** Moray
2 C5 **Cairngarroch** D & G
56 B5 **Cairngorm Mountains** Abers
67 K5 **Cairnie** Abers
69 G6 **Cairnorrie** Abers
2 C2 **Cairnryan** D & G
67 H4 **Cairnty** Moray
84 e2 **Calanais** W Isls
67 G2 **Calcots** Moray
27 K5 **Calderbank** N Lans
27 L5 **Caldercruix** N Lans
16 D2 **Caldermill** S Lans
27 H7 **Calderwood** S Lans
86 d4 **Calfsound** Ork
41 J6 **Calgary** Ag & B

66 D3 **Califer** Moray
28 B3 **California** Falk
61 L4 **Callakille** Highld
36 D5 **Callander** Stirlg
84 e2 **Callanish** W Isls
51 K5 **Calligarry** Highld
46 C3 **Calvine** P & K
17 L3 **Calzeat** Border
42 F4 **Camasachoirce** Highld
42 F4 **Camasine** Highld
62 E8 **Camas Luinie** Highld
61 H6 **Camastianavaig** Highld
64 D6 **Camault Muir** Highld
37 H8 **Cambus** Clacks
75 G3 **Cambusavie Platform** Highld
37 G8 **Cambusbarron** Stirlg
37 G8 **Cambuskenneth** Stirlg
27 H6 **Cambuslang** S Lans
57 J5 **Cambus o' May** Abers
17 K2 **Cambuswallace** S Lans
28 B3 **Camelon** Falk
66 C7 **Camerory** Highld
45 J5 **Camghouran** P & K
19 J4 **Camieston** Border
59 G6 **Cammachmore** Abers
75 G4 **Camore** Highld
13 J5 **Campbeltown** Ag & B
13 H5 *Campbeltown Airport* Ag & B
8 F4 **Cample** D & G
47 K8 **Campmuir** P & K
28 E5 **Camps** W Loth
19 K6 **Camptown** Border
46 C6 **Camserney** P & K
43 L2 **Camusnagaul** Highld
72 D4 **Camusnagaul** Highld
61 L6 **Camusteel** Highld
61 L6 **Camusterrach** Highld
57 H5 **Candacraig** Abers
17 L2 **Candy Mill** Border
83 L2 **Canisbay** Highld
50 C4 **Canna** Highld
63 L7 **Cannich** Highld
10 C6 **Canonbie** D & G
65 J5 **Cantraywood** Highld
43 L2 **Caol** Highld
84 e4 **Caolas Scalpaigh** W Isls
40 D6 **Caoles** Ag & B
53 G6 **Caonich** Highld
26 E6 **Caplaw** E Rens
18 C5 **Cappercleuch** Border
47 H7 **Caputh** P & K
26 F3 **Carbeth Inn** Stirlg
60 F5 **Carbost** Highld
60 F7 **Carbost** Highld

38 C7 **Cardenden** Fife
66 F5 **Cardhu** Moray
2 D8 **Cardrain** D & G
18 D2 **Cardrona** Border
26 C3 **Cardross** Ag & B
2 D7 **Cardryne** D & G
48 E4 **Careston** Angus
27 K6 **Carfin** N Lans
30 B7 **Carfraemill** Border
9 G6 **Cargenbridge** D & G
47 J8 **Cargill** P & K
45 K5 **Carie** P & K
85 c6 **Carinish** W Isls
84 e2 **Carlabhagh** W Isls
68 D5 **Carlincraig** Abers
29 G6 **Carlops** Border
84 e2 **Carloway** W Isls
27 L7 **Carluke** S Lans
16 F4 **Carmacoup** S Lans
17 H2 **Carmichael** S Lans
27 G6 **Carmunnock** C Glas
27 H6 **Carmyle** C Glas
48 E7 **Carmyllie** Angus
39 J6 **Carnbee** Fife
37 L6 **Carnbo** P & K
68 F8 **Carnbrogie** Abers
62 D8 **Carndu** Highld
16 D1 **Carnduff** S Lans
15 L3 **Carnell** E Ayrs
52 E2 **Carn-gorm** Highld
58 F4 **Carnie** Abers
52 D6 **Carnoch** Highld
28 E1 **Carnock** Fife
68 C4 **Carnousie** Abers
39 J1 **Carnoustie** Angus
17 J1 **Carnwath** S Lans
13 K2 **Carradale** Ag & B
55 L2 **Carrbridge** Highld
24 F2 **Carrick** Ag & B
35 H8 **Carrick Castle** Ag & B
28 D3 **Carriden** Falk
29 J6 **Carrington** Mdloth
28 B2 **Carron** Falk
66 F6 **Carron** Moray
8 F3 **Carronbridge** D & G
27 K2 **Carron Bridge** Stirlg
28 B2 **Carronshore** Falk
9 J7 **Carrutherstown** D & G
26 C5 **Carruth House** Inver
33 H3 **Carsaig** Ag & B
48 D5 **Carse Gray** Angus
3 G2 **Carseriggan** D & G
5 H3 **Carsethorn** D & G
13 H7 **Carskey** Ag & B
3 K4 **Carsluith** D & G
7 L4 **Carsphairn** D & G
17 H1 **Carstairs** S Lans
17 J1 **Carstairs Junction** S Lans
17 G1 **Cartland** S Lans
85 b9 **Castlebay** W Isls
27 K3 **Castlecary** Falk
4 D3 **Castle Douglas** D & G
18 C3 **Castlehill** Border
83 H2 **Castlehill** Highld
26 D3 **Castlehill** W Duns
2 D3 **Castle Kennedy** D & G

34 E7 **Castle Lachlan** Ag & B
27 G6 **Castlemilk** C Glas
10 A4 **Castle O'er** D & G
65 H4 **Castle Stuart** Highld
10 E4 **Castleton** Border
83 H3 **Castletown** Highld
24 F7 **Catacol** N Ayrs
27 G6 **Cathcart** C Glas
54 F6 **Catlodge** Highld
16 B4 **Catrine** E Ayrs
13 H7 **Cattadale** Ag & B
49 L2 **Catterline** Abers
49 G6 **Cauldcots** Angus
36 E8 **Cauldhame** Stirlg
19 H6 **Cauldmill** Border
5 G4 **Caulkerbush** D & G
10 D6 **Caulside** D & G
3 J3 **Causeway End** D & G
17 K3 **Causewayend** S Lans
37 G7 **Causewayhead** Stirlg
59 H2 **Causeyend** Abers
19 L4 **Caverton Mill** Border
65 K4 **Cawdor** Highld
85 b6 **Ceann a Bhaigh** W Isls
53 K3 **Ceannacroc Lodge** Highld
84 f3 **Cearsiadar** W Isls
39 J6 **Cellardyke** Fife
38 F5 **Ceres** Fife
3 H2 **Challoch** D & G
38 D8 **Chapel** Fife
27 K5 **Chapelhall** N Lans
69 K7 **Chapel Hill** Abers
18 C5 **Chapelhope** Border
10 B7 **Chapelknowe** D & G
58 D1 **Chapel of Garioch** Abers
2 D6 **Chapel Rossan** D & G
49 G6 **Chapelton** Angus
27 J8 **Chapelton** S Lans
56 F2 **Chapeltown** Moray
48 C7 **Charleston** Angus
59 H5 **Charlestown** C Aber
28 E2 **Charlestown** Fife
65 G5 **Charlestown** Highld
71 J6 **Charlestown** Highld
38 E5 **Charlottetown** Fife
31 G8 **Charterhall** Border
27 K1 **Chartershall** Stirlg
20 B5 **Chatto** Border
29 K5 **Chesterhill** Mdloth
19 J5 **Chesters** Border
19 K7 **Chesters** Border
20 A7 **Cheviot Hills** Border
31 H6 **Chirnside** Border
31 H7 **Chirnsidebridge** Border
18 F6 **Chisholme** Border
2 D3 **Chlenry** D & G
25 L4 **Chrisswell** Inver
40 F5 **Clabhach** Ag & B
25 J3 **Clachaig** Ag & B
24 C6 **Clachan** Ag & B
34 A4 **Clachan** Ag & B
43 G7 **Clachan** Ag & B

61 H6 **Clachan** Highld
85 c6 **Clachan-a-Luib** W Isls
40 C6 **Clachan Mor** Ag & B
85 c6 **Clachan na Luib** W Isls
27 G3 **Clachan of Campsie** E Duns
33 M4 **Clachan-Seil** Ag & B
65 G5 **Clachnaharry** Highld
76 C3 **Clachtoll** Highld
47 J4 **Clackavoid** P & K
37 J8 **Clackmannan** Clacks
66 F3 **Clackmarras** Moray
34 F3 **Cladich** Ag & B
42 E6 **Claggan** Highld
60 C4 **Claigan** Highld
24 E6 **Claonaig** Ag & B
4 D2 **Clarebrand** D & G
5 J2 **Clarencefield** D & G
19 H5 **Clarilaw** Border
27 G6 **Clarkston** E Rens
75 G4 **Clashmore** Highld
76 C3 **Clashmore** Highld
76 C3 **Clashnessie** Highld
56 F2 **Clashnoir** Moray
37 K4 **Clathy** P & K
37 L3 **Clathymore** P & K
57 L1 **Clatt** Abers
10 D6 **Claygate** D & G
83 H4 **Clayock** Highld
51 G7 **Cleadale** Highld
86 C8 **Cleat** Ork
27 K6 **Cleekhimin** N Lans
30 D2 **Cleghornie** E Loth
38 A7 **Cleish** P & K
27 L6 **Cleland** N Lans
34 C2 **Clenamacrie** Ag & B
68 E3 **Clenerty** Abers
13 H3 **Cleongart** Ag & B
65 J4 **Clephanton** Highld
10 A3 **Clerkhill** D & G
8 E3 **Cleuch-head** D & G
58 F3 **Clinterty** C Aber
19 J3 **Clintmains** Border
67 J3 **Clochan** Moray
48 D5 **Clochtow** Angus
69 J5 **Clola** Abers
8 F4 **Closeburn** D & G
8 F3 **Closeburnmill** D & G
87 c5 **Clousta** Shet
48 B2 **Clova** Angus
19 G3 **Clovenfords** Border
43 K4 **Clovulin** Highld
53 G3 **Cluanie Inn** Highld
53 G3 **Cluanie Lodge** Highld
3 H4 **Clugston** D & G
65 K5 **Clunas** Highld
55 J1 **Clune** Highld
53 J7 **Clunes** Highld
68 C4 **Clunie** Abers
47 H7 **Clunie** P & K
38 D7 **Cluny** Fife
26 F4 **Clydebank** W Duns
26 A2 **Clynder** Ag & B
84 g2 **Cnoc** W Isls
16 F3 **Coalburn** S Lans
37 J7 **Coalsnaughton** Clacks

38 E7 **Coaltown of Balgonie** Fife
38 E7 **Coaltown of Wemyss** Fife
27 J5 **Coatbridge** N Lans
27 K5 **Coatdyke** N Lans
69 H2 **Coburby** Abers
57 G4 **Cock Bridge** Abers
31 G4 **Cockburnspath** Border
29 L4 **Cockenzie and Port Seton** E Loth
55 H4 **Coignafearn** Highld
57 H6 **Coilacriech** Abers
36 D6 **Coilantogle** Stirlg
60 E6 **Coillore** Highld
84 g2 **Col** W Isls
77 L6 **Colaboll** Highld
60 C5 **Colbost** Highld
81 J4 **Coldbackie** Highld
31 J5 **Coldingham** Border
20 C2 **Coldstream** Border
69 H6 **Coldwells** Abers
38 B2 **Colenden** P & K
39 H6 **Colinsburgh** Fife
29 H5 **Colinton** C Edin
25 H4 **Colintraive** Ag & B
41 G5 **Coll** Ag & B
38 C2 **Collace** P & K
87 c3 **Collafirth** Shet
66 E2 **College of Roseisle** Moray
38 E5 **Collessie** Fife
69 K8 **Collieston** Abers
9 H6 **Collin** D & G
48 F7 **Colliston** Angus
6 D5 **Colmonell** S Ayrs
32 E7 **Colonsay** Ag & B
68 C7 **Colpy** Abers
18 E2 **Colquhar** Border
66 D2 **Coltfield** Moray
4 F4 **Colvend** D & G
58 D4 **Comers** Abers
4 B4 **Compstonend** D & G
28 D1 **Comrie** Fife
37 G3 **Comrie** P & K
43 K3 **Conaglen House** Highld
62 D8 **Conchra** Highld
47 H7 **Concraigie** P & K
27 K4 **Condorrat** N Lans
5 H2 **Conheath** D & G
66 B4 **Conicavel** Moray
34 C1 **Connel** Ag & B
16 C6 **Connel Park** E Ayrs
64 E4 **Conon Bridge** Highld
64 C3 **Contin** Highld
59 G6 **Cookney** Abers
87 d3 **Copister** Shet
14 D4 **Cordon** N Ayrs
57 K4 **Corgarff** Abers
47 L3 **Cormuir** Angus
68 B3 **Cornhill** Abers
40 C6 **Cornoigmore** Ag & B
64 E3 **Corntown** Highld
43 L2 **Corpach** Highld
57 K4 **Corrachree** Abers
43 K4 **Corran** Highld
52 C4 **Corran** Highld

9 L5 **Corrie** D & G
14 C2 **Corrie** N Ayrs
14 B5 **Corriecravie** N Ayrs
14 D3 **Corriegills** N Ayrs
53 K6 **Corriegour Lodge Hotel** Highld
64 B2 **Corriemoille** Highld
64 B7 **Corrimony** Highld
35 H7 **Corrow** Ag & B
51 K1 **Corry** Highld
58 D4 **Corsindae** Abers
8 D6 **Corsock** D & G
29 G4 **Corstorphine** C Edin
48 C4 **Cortachy** Angus
43 L3 **Coruanan** Highld
46 C6 **Coshieville** P & K
59 G3 **Cothal** Abers
58 E3 **Cottown** Abers
67 L8 **Cottown** Abers
68 F6 **Cottown of Gight** Abers
24 C5 **Coulaghailtro** Ag & B
62 E5 **Coulags** Highld
57 L5 **Coull** Abers
25 L2 **Coulport** Ag & B
17 K3 **Coulter** S Lans
38 F3 **Coultra** Fife
47 K7 **Coupar Angus** P & K
24 D8 **Cour** Ag & B
51 L6 **Courteachan** Highld
29 K5 **Cousland** Mdloth
25 L2 **Cove** Ag & B
31 G4 **Cove** Border
71 J3 **Cove** Highld
59 H5 **Cove Bay** C Aber
17 J2 **Covington** S Lans
29 G1 **Cowdenbeath** Fife
27 L1 **Cowie** Stirlg
15 K5 **Coylton** S Ayrs
55 L3 **Coylumbridge** Highld
56 C1 **Craggan** Highld
67 L3 **Craibstone** Moray
48 E6 **Craichie** Angus
49 H5 **Craig** Angus
63 G4 **Craig** Highld
16 C6 **Craigbank** E Ayrs
29 H7 **Craigburn** Border
10 C5 **Craigcleuch** D & G
68 F7 **Craigdam** Abers
34 B6 **Craigdhu** Ag & B
58 D3 **Craigearn** Abers
67 G5 **Craigellachie** Moray
38 B4 **Craigend** P & K
26 E4 **Craigend** Rens
26 C3 **Craigendoran** Ag & B
26 D5 **Craigends** Rens
3 G3 **Craighlaw** D & G
23 K5 **Craighouse** Ag & B
47 H7 **Craigie** P & K
15 K3 **Craigie** S Ayrs
69 H2 **Craigiefold** Abers
4 D4 **Craigley** D & G
29 H4 **Craiglockhart** C Edin
29 J4 **Craigmillar** C Edin
8 D5 **Craigneston** D & G
27 K5 **Craigneuk** N Lans
27 K6 **Craigneuk** N Lans

42 E8 **Craignure** Ag & B
49 H4 **Craigo** Angus
38 F5 **Craigrothie** Fife
36 B4 **Craigruie** Stirlg
48 E8 **Craigton** Angus
58 F5 **Craigton** C Aber
26 F7 **Craigton** E Rens
48 B6 **Craigton of Airlie** Angus
39 K5 **Crail** Fife
19 L4 **Crailing** Border
29 G3 **Cramond** C Edin
29 G4 **Cramond Bridge** C Edin
30 E6 **Cranshaws** Border
34 A6 **Craobh Haven** Ag & B
34 E7 **Crarae** Ag & B
77 L4 **Crask Inn** Highld
64 D6 **Crask of Aigas** Highld
58 E6 **Crathes** Abers
58 D6 **Crathes Castle** Abers
57 G6 **Crathie** Abers
54 E6 **Crathie** Highld
17 J5 **Crawford** S Lans
17 G5 **Crawfordjohn** S Lans
49 L1 **Crawton** Abers
43 J7 **Creagan Inn** Ag & B
85 c7 **Creag Ghoraidh** W Isls
85 c7 **Creagorry** W Isls
44 E3 **Creaguaineach Lodge** Highld
9 M7 **Creca** D & G
7 H6 **Creebank** D & G
3 J2 **Creebridge** D & G
3 K3 **Creetown** D & G
38 E3 **Creich** Fife
24 C5 **Cretshengan** Ag & B
35 L3 **Crianlarich** Stirlg
29 K6 **Crichton** Mdloth
37 H3 **Crieff** P & K
69 K3 **Crimond** Abers
64 C6 **Crinaglack** Highld
34 A8 **Crinan** Ag & B
27 L6 **Crindledyke** N Lans
65 G8 **Croachy** Highld
8 E7 **Crocketford** D & G
26 E2 **Croftamie** Stirlg
72 F5 **Croftown** Highld
67 G4 **Crofts** Moray
67 H3 **Crofts of Dipple** Moray
69 K3 **Crofts of Savoch** Abers
33 L3 **Croggan** Ag & B
74 B3 **Croick** Highld
75 H7 **Cromarty** Highld
28 E2 **Crombie** Fife
66 D8 **Cromdale** Highld
84 f3 **Cromor** W Isls
16 C5 **Cronberry** E Ayrs
15 L3 **Crookedholm** E Ayrs
17 L4 **Crook Inn** Border
37 L7 **Crook of Devon** P & K
84 g1 **Cros** W Isls

25 L7 **Crosbie** N Ayrs
84 f3 **Crosbost** W Isls
24 E7 **Crossaig** Ag & B
40 C7 **Crossapoll** Ag & B
28 E2 **Crossford** Fife
27 L8 **Crossford** S Lans
29 K5 **Crossgatehall** E Loth
15 J1 **Crossgates** E Ayrs
28 F1 **Crossgates** Fife
15 L4 **Crosshands** E Ayrs
38 C7 **Crosshill** Fife
15 J7 **Crosshill** S Ayrs
15 K2 **Crosshouse** E Ayrs
26 C2 **Cross Keys** Ag & B
82 F7 **Crosskirk** Highld
26 D5 **Crosslee** Rens
4 C2 **Crossmichael** D & G
68 E7 **Cross of Jackston** Abers
58 B4 **Crossroads** Abers
58 E6 **Crossroads** Abers
48 E5 **Crosston** Angus
68 F2 **Crovie** Abers
30 F4 **Crowhill** E Loth
65 J4 **Croy** Highld
27 J3 **Croy** N Lans
55 G7 **Crubenmore** Highld
69 K6 **Cruden Bay** Abers
61 L3 **Cruaig** Highld
33 L4 **Cuan Ferry Village** Ag & B
43 J5 **Cuil** Highld
64 F3 **Culbokie** Highld
64 D6 **Culburnie** Highld
65 G5 **Culcabock** Highld
65 K4 **Culcharry** Highld
67 L7 **Culdrain** Abers
61 L6 **Culduie** Highld
76 C2 **Culkein** Highld
76 D2 **Culkein Drumbeg** Highld
67 L2 **Cullen** Moray
58 E5 **Cullerlie** Abers
65 G2 **Cullicudden** Highld
51 G2 **Cuillin Hills** Highld
33 L5 **Cullipool House** Ag & B
87 d2 **Cullivoe** Shet
65 H5 **Culloden** Highld
76 C7 **Culnacraig** Highld
4 D5 **Culnaightrie** D & G
61 H2 **Culnaknock** Highld
74 D3 **Culrain** Highld
28 D2 **Culross** Fife
15 H6 **Culroy** S Ayrs
68 C7 **Culsalmond** Abers
3 K5 **Culscadden** D & G
3 G5 **Culshabbin** D & G
87 b6 **Culswick** Shet
59 H1 **Cultercullen** Abers
59 G5 **Cults** C Aber
15 G7 **Culzean Castle** S Ayrs
27 K4 **Cumbernauld** N Lans
27 K4 **Cumbernauld Village** N Lans
68 F4 **Cuminestown** Abers
31 G6 **Cumledge** Border
5 K2 **Cummertrees** D & G

66 E1 **Cummingston** Moray
16 B5 **Cumnock** E Ayrs
9 J5 **Cumrue** D & G
15 J2 **Cunninghamhead** N Ayrs
87 c7 **Cunningsburgh** Shet
38 F4 **Cupar** Fife
38 F5 **Cupar Muir** Fife
29 G5 **Currie** C Edin
57 L3 **Cushnie** Abers
3 J7 **Cutcloy** D & G
75 G4 **Cuthill** Highld

D

6 F2 **Dailly** S Ayrs
39 G4 **Dairsie** Fife
85 b8 **Dalabrog** W Isls
34 D5 **Dalavich** Ag & B
4 E3 **Dalbeattie** D & G
46 F5 **Dalcapon** P & K
78 F7 **Dalchalm** Highld
53 L3 **Dalchreichart** Highld
36 F4 **Dalchruin** P & K
37 L2 **Dalcrue** P & K
42 E3 **Dalelia** Highld
15 H1 **Dalgarven** N Ayrs
29 G2 **Dalgety Bay** Fife
16 B6 **Dalgig** E Ayrs
37 G3 **Dalginross** P & K
46 F6 **Dalguise** P & K
82 C5 **Dalhalvaig** Highld
85 b8 **Daliburgh** W Isls
29 K5 **Dalkeith** Mdloth
66 D4 **Dallas** Moray
35 H3 **Dalmally** Ag & B
36 C7 **Dalmary** Stirlg
7 K2 **Dalmellington** E Ayrs
28 F3 **Dalmeny** C Edin
55 H2 **Dalmigavie** Highld
55 H2 **Dalmigavie Lodge** Highld
74 F7 **Dalmore** Highld
26 E4 **Dalmuir** W Duns
42 E3 **Dalnabreck** Highld
46 B3 **Dalnacardoch** P & K
55 K2 **Dalnahaitnach** Highld
45 K2 **Dalnaspidal** P & K
82 F7 **Dalnawillan Lodge** Highld
46 C5 **Daloist** P & K
38 A6 **Dalqueich** P & K
7 G3 **Dalquhairn** S Ayrs
78 D6 **Dalreavoch Lodge** Highld
26 B7 **Dalry** N Ayrs
15 J6 **Dalrymple** E Ayrs
27 L7 **Dalserf** S Lans
13 G6 **Dalsmeran** Ag & B
9 G5 **Dalswinton** D & G
9 K7 **Dalton** D & G
17 G7 **Dalveen** D & G
36 D3 **Dalveich** Stirlg
54 F7 **Dalwhinnie** Highld
67 G5 **Dandaleith** Moray

29 J4 **Danderhall** Mdloth
68 D3 **Danshillock** Abers
30 C5 **Danskine** E Loth
19 H3 **Darnick** Border
68 E5 **Darra** Abers
16 B2 **Darvel** E Ayrs
66 F6 **Daugh of Kinermony** Moray
66 C6 **Dava** Highld
29 G4 **Davidson's Mains** C Edin
9 M2 **Davington** D & G
68 E8 **Daviot** Abers
65 H6 **Daviot** Highld
65 H6 **Daviot House** Highld
67 K4 **Davoch of Grange** Moray
18 F6 **Deanburnhaugh** Border
28 D5 **Deans** W Loth
67 H4 **Deanshaugh** Moray
36 F6 **Deanston** Stirlg
28 E4 **Dechmont** W Loth
28 D4 **Dechmont Road** W Loth
34 A5 **Degnish** Ag & B
59 H2 **Delfrigs** Abers
66 D7 **Delliefure** Highld
56 E3 **Delnabo** Moray
66 E7 **Delnashaugh Inn** Moray
75 G6 **Delny** Highld
47 H7 **Delvine** P & K
38 F4 **Denbrae** Fife
37 K4 **Denfield** P & K
69 J4 **Denhead** Abers
39 G5 **Denhead** Fife
38 F2 **Denhead of Gray** C Dund
19 J5 **Denholm** Border
59 H3 **Denmore** C Aber
27 L2 **Denny** Falk
27 L3 **Dennyloanhead** Falk
38 D4 **Den of Lindores** Fife
58 F6 **Denside** Abers
46 D5 **Derculich** P & K
41 K6 **Dervaig** Ag & B
67 L3 **Deskford** Moray
37 J7 **Devonside** Clacks
29 K5 **Dewarton** Mdloth
70 C7 **Digg** Highld
64 E3 **Dingwall** Highld
57 K5 **Dinnet** Abers
9 K4 **Dinwoodie** D & G
13 K2 **Dippen** Ag & B
14 D5 **Dippen** N Ayrs
67 H3 **Dipple** Moray
6 E2 **Dipple** S Ayrs
30 B2 **Dirleton** E Loth
64 F6 **Dochgarroch** Highld
26 F7 **Dodside** E Rens
78 F7 **Doll** Highld
37 K7 **Dollar** Clacks
37 K7 **Dollarfield** Clacks
28 F8 **Dolphinton** S Lans
29 G2 **Donibristle** Fife
15 H5 **Doonfoot** S Ayrs
15 J6 **Doonholm** S Ayrs

56 D3 **Dorback Lodge** Highld
64 F7 **Dores** Highld
52 D1 **Dornie** Highld
75 H4 **Dornoch** Highld
5 M2 **Dornock** D & G
82 F5 **Dorrery** Highld
17 G4 **Douglas** S Lans
39 G2 **Douglas and Angus** C Dund
17 G3 **Douglas Castle** S Lans
35 H7 **Douglas Pier** Ag & B
48 C6 **Douglastown** Angus
17 G3 **Douglas Water** S Lans
16 F3 **Douglas West** S Lans
86 b5 **Dounby** Ork
73 L2 **Doune** Highld
36 F6 **Doune** Stirlg
6 E3 **Dounepark** S Ayrs
74 D4 **Dounie** Highld
46 F6 **Dowally** P & K
38 F2 **Downfield** C Dund
38 A2 **Downhill** P & K
59 H6 **Downies** Abers
16 F1 **Draffan** S Lans
26 B7 **Drakemyre** N Ayrs
15 J2 **Dreghorn** N Ayrs
30 B3 **Drem** E Loth
42 B5 **Drimnin** Highld
43 J1 **Drimsallie** Highld
38 B4 **Dron** P & K
15 K5 **Drongan** E Ayrs
38 E1 **Dronley** Angus
43 L3 **Druimarbin** Highld
43 K7 **Druimavuic** Ag & B
24 C4 **Druimdrishaig** Ag & B
51 L7 **Druimindarroch** Highld
24 F3 **Drum** Ag & B
37 L7 **Drum** P & K
17 H2 **Drumalbin** S Lans
76 D3 **Drumbeg** Highld
68 B6 **Drumblade** Abers
2 C6 **Drumbreddon** D & G
62 B7 **Drumbuie** Highld
4 F4 **Drumburn** D & G
26 F4 **Drumchapel** C Glas
45 L5 **Drumchastle** P & K
16 C2 **Drumclog** S Lans
39 G6 **Drumeldrie** Fife
17 M3 **Drumelzier** Border
51 L3 **Drumfearn** Highld
58 D5 **Drumfrennie** Abers
48 C6 **Drumgley** Angus
55 J5 **Drumguish** Highld
66 E7 **Drumin** Moray
7 L3 **Drumjohn** D & G
7 G6 **Drumlamford** S Ayrs
58 C4 **Drumlasie** Abers
13 H5 **Drumlemble** Ag & B
49 J1 **Drumlithie** Abers
3 H6 **Drummoddie** D & G
2 D7 **Drummore** D & G
67 J5 **Drummuir** Moray

64 D7 **Drumnadrochit** Highld
2 D7 **Drumnaglaur** D & G
67 L4 **Drumnagorrach** Moray
8 F6 **Drumpark** D & G
76 E7 **Drumrunie Lodge** Highld
15 G6 **Drumshang** S Ayrs
61 G3 **Drumuie** Highld
56 B2 **Drumuillie** Highld
38 E6 **Drumvaich** Stirlg
38 B5 **Drunzie** P & K
67 K2 **Drybridge** Moray
15 J3 **Drybridge** N Ayrs
19 J3 **Dryburgh** Border
26 E2 **Drymen** Stirlg
69 G5 **Drymuir** Abers
60 F7 **Drynoch** Highld
68 F2 **Dubford** Abers
77 J5 **Duchally** Highld
29 J4 **Duddingston** C Edin
67 H6 **Dufftown** Moray
66 E2 **Duffus** Moray
62 B7 **Duirinish** Highld
51 L3 **Duisdalemore** Highld
43 K2 **Duisky** Highld
46 C6 **Dull** P & K
27 K3 **Dullatur** N Lans
56 B1 **Dulnain Bridge** Highld
26 D4 **Dumbarton** W Duns
9 G6 **Dumfries** D & G
26 F2 **Dumgoyne** Stirlg
49 G4 **Dun** Angus
45 L5 **Dunalastair** P & K
25 K4 **Dunan** Ag & B
61 J8 **Dunan** Highld
45 G3 **Dunan** P & K
13 H7 **Dunaverty** Ag & B
30 E3 **Dunbar** E Loth
79 M3 **Dunbeath** Highld
34 C2 **Dunbeg** Ag & B
37 G6 **Dunblane** Stirlg
38 E4 **Dunbog** Fife
64 F3 **Duncanston** Highld
68 B8 **Duncanstone** Abers
9 G5 **Duncow** D & G
38 B5 **Duncrievie** P & K
38 F2 **Dundee** C Dund
38 F2 *Dundee Airport* C Dund
15 J3 **Dundonald** S Ayrs
72 E4 **Dundonnell** Highld
53 L3 **Dundreggan** Highld
4 D5 **Dundrennan** D & G
58 E4 **Dunecht** Abers
28 F2 **Dunfermline** Fife
16 D3 **Dungavel** S Lans
39 J5 **Dunino** Fife
27 L2 **Dunipace** Falk
47 G7 **Dunkeld** P & K
48 F3 **Dunlappie** Angus
26 D8 **Dunlop** E Ayrs
54 F2 **Dunmaglass** Highld
28 B1 **Dunmore** Falk
83 J2 **Dunnet** Highld
48 E6 **Dunnichen** Angus
37 L4 **Dunning** P & K
25 K3 **Dunoon** Ag & B
66 C5 **Dunphail** Moray

2 E4 **Dunragit** D & G
31 G7 **Duns** Border
8 F5 **Dunscore** D & G
38 D5 **Dunshalt** Fife
69 J5 **Dunshillock** Abers
28 E8 **Dunsyre** S Lans
26 E4 **Duntocher** W Duns
70 C6 **Duntulm** Highld
15 G6 **Dunure** S Ayrs
60 D5 **Dunvegan** Highld
8 F2 **Durisdeer** D & G
8 F2 **Durisdeermill** D & G
80 F3 **Durness** Highld
68 D8 **Durno** Abers
43 K5 **Duror** Highld
34 D5 **Durran** Ag & B
58 E6 **Durris** Abers
55 L1 **Duthil** Highld
59 G3 **Dyce** C Aber
66 B3 **Dyke** Moray
47 K5 **Dykehead** Angus
48 C4 **Dykehead** Angus
28 B6 **Dykehead** N Lans
36 D7 **Dykehead** Stirlg
49 H3 **Dykelands** Abers
47 K5 **Dykends** Angus
68 D5 **Dykeside** Abers
38 E8 **Dysart** Fife

E

9 M7 **Eaglesfield** D & G
27 G7 **Eaglesham** E Rens
60 F3 **Earlish** Highld
39 H7 **Earlsferry** Fife
68 F7 **Earlsford** Abers
19 J2 **Earlston** Border
15 K3 **Earlston** E Ayrs
33 L4 **Easdale** Ag & B
48 B7 **Eassie and Nevay** Angus
30 F3 **East Barns** E Loth
28 E5 **East Calder** W Loth
57 G6 **Easter Balmoral** Abers
65 H4 **Easter Dalziel** Highld
27 J5 **Easterhouse** C Glas
29 H5 **Easter Howgate** Mdloth
64 E4 **Easter Kinkell** Highld
64 E5 **Easter Moniack** Highld
58 F4 **Easter Ord** Abers
39 J6 **Easter Pitkierie** Fife
87 c6 **Easter Skeld** Shet
20 A3 **Easter Softlaw** Border
28 B5 **Eastfield** N Lans
30 C3 **East Fortune** E Loth
39 J1 **East Haven** Angus
79 H5 **East Helmsdale** Highld
27 H7 **East Kilbride** S Lans
8 E7 **Eastlands** D & G
43 L5 **East Laroch** Highld
30 D3 **East Linton** E Loth
8 F3 **East Morton** D & G
5 M2 **Eastriggs** D & G
30 B5 **East Saltoun** E Loth

38 E7 **East Wemyss** Fife
28 C5 **East Whitburn** W Loth
30 F5 **Ecclaw** Border
9 L7 **Ecclefechan** D & G
20 A2 **Eccles** Border
28 E4 **Ecclesmachan** W Loth
58 E4 **Echt** Abers
19 L4 **Eckford** Border
86 d4 **Eday** Ork
86 d4 *Eday Airport* Ork
74 F4 **Edderton** Highld
29 H8 **Eddleston** Border
27 J7 **Eddlewood** S Lans
35 K8 **Edentaggart** Ag & B
60 E4 **Edinbane** Highld
29 H4 **Edinburgh** C Edin
28 F4 *Edinburgh Airport* C Edin
29 H4 **Edinburgh Castle** C Edin
29 H4 **Edinburgh Royal Botanic Gardens** C Edin
29 G4 **Edinburgh Zoo** C Edin
4 E3 **Edingham** D & G
31 J7 **Edington** Border
19 L2 **Ednam** Border
46 D6 **Edradynate** P & K
31 H7 **Edrom** Border
48 F3 **Edzell** Angus
49 G3 **Edzell Woods** Abers
10 B4 **Effgill** D & G
51 G7 **Eigg** Highld
52 C2 **Eilanreach** Highld
26 E5 **Elderslie** Rens
58 F7 **Elfhill** Abers
66 F2 **Elgin** Moray
51 H3 **Elgol** Highld
39 H7 **Elie** Fife
68 C3 **Ella** Abers
33 L4 **Ellanbeich** Ag & B
24 C3 **Ellary** Ag & B
30 F6 **Ellemford** Border
43 K6 **Elleric** Ag & B
61 H2 **Ellishader** Highld
69 H7 **Ellon** Abers
76 F6 **Elphin** Highld
29 K4 **Elphinstone** E Loth
58 F4 **Elrick** Abers
3 G5 **Elrig** D & G
17 K2 **Elsrickle** S Lans
17 J6 **Elvanfoot** S Lans
30 A4 **Elvingston** E Loth
75 H3 **Embo** Highld
75 H3 **Embo Street** Highld
47 G4 **Enochdhu** P & K
41 J6 **Ensay** Ag & B
8 E2 **Enterkinfoot** D & G
85 b9 **Eolaigearraidh** W Isls
24 E4 **Erines** Ag & B
43 H7 **Eriska** Ag & B
85 c9 **Eriskay** W Isls
54 E2 **Errogie** Highld
38 D3 **Errol** P & K
26 E4 **Erskine** Rens
2 B2 **Ervie** D & G
64 C6 **Eskadale** Highld
29 J5 **Eskbank** Mdloth

10 A3 **Eskdalemuir** D & G
65 G6 **Essich** Highld
69 H7 **Esslemont** Abers
55 G6 **Etteridge** Highld
18 D6 **Ettrick** Border
18 F4 **Ettrickbridge** Border
18 C6 **Ettrickhill** Border
64 F2 **Evanton** Highld
75 G4 **Evelix** Highld
10 C6 **Evertown** D & G
31 K5 **Eyemouth** Border
60 F4 **Eyre** Highld

F

26 F4 **Faifley** W Duns
15 L4 **Failford** S Ayrs
4 F4 **Fairgirth** D & G
87 e7 **Fair Isle** Shet
25 L7 **Fairlie** N Ayrs
19 G3 **Fairnilee** Border
29 L6 **Fala** Mdloth
29 L6 **Fala Dam** Mdloth
29 L7 **Falahill** Border
28 B3 **Falkirk** Falk
38 D6 **Falkland** Fife
17 J2 **Fallburn** S Lans
37 H8 **Fallin** Stirlg
34 E5 **Falls of Blarghour** Ag & B
10 D2 **Falnash** Border
80 B5 **Fanagmore** Highld
64 D5 **Fanellan** Highld
41 K7 **Fanmore** Ag & B
63 K2 **Fannich Lodge** Highld
19 J2 **Fans** Border
37 L1 **Farkhill** P & K
67 L4 **Farmtown** Moray
49 G5 **Farnell** Angus
55 K5 **Farr** Highld
65 G7 **Farr** Highld
81 L3 **Farr** Highld
54 E2 **Farraline** Highld
43 K6 **Fasnacloich** Ag & B
63 L8 **Fasnakyle** Highld
43 K2 **Fassfern** Highld
28 C6 **Fauldhouse** W Loth
75 H6 **Fearn** Highld
46 B7 **Fearnan** P & K
62 B3 **Fearnbeg** Highld
61 L3 **Fearnmore** Highld
24 F3 **Fearnoch** Ag & B
30 B3 **Fenton Barns** E Loth
15 L2 **Fenwick** E Ayrs
23 H4 **Feolin Ferry** Ag & B
15 J2 **Fergushill** N Ayrs
60 B4 **Feriniquarrie** Highld
48 D4 **Fern** Angus
66 B5 **Ferness** Highld
38 E4 **Fernie** Fife
27 K7 **Ferniegair** S Lans
60 F7 **Fernilea** Highld
51 K4 **Ferrindonald** Highld
49 H5 **Ferryden** Angus
75 G4 **Ferry Point** Highld
75 G4 **Ferrytown** Highld

44 F2 **Fersit** Highld
55 K4 **Feshiebridge** Highld
87 e2 **Fetlar** Shet
69 J4 **Fetterangus** Abers
49 G2 **Fettercairn** Abers
77 K3 **Fiag Lodge** Highld
67 J4 **Fife Keith** Moray
48 D5 **Finavon** Angus
34 C6 **Fincharn** Ag & B
66 C2 **Findhorn** Moray
65 J8 **Findhorn Bridge** Highld
67 K2 **Findochty** Moray
37 L4 **Findo Gask** P & K
59 H6 **Findon** Abers
64 F3 **Findon Mains** Highld
58 B4 **Findrack House** Abers
38 C4 **Fingask** P & K
16 E6 **Fingland** D & G
36 C1 **Finlarig** Stirlg
45 H5 **Finnart** P & K
84 d5 **Finsbay** W Isls
86 b6 **Finstown** Ork
68 E4 **Fintry** Abers
27 H2 **Fintry** Stirlg
58 B6 **Finzean** Abers
32 D3 **Fionnphort** Ag & B
84 d5 **Fionnsbhagh** W Isls
37 J7 **Fishcross** Clacks
68 C7 **Fisherford** Abers
29 K4 **Fisherrow** E Loth
65 H4 **Fisherton** Highld
15 H6 **Fisherton** S Ayrs
42 D7 **Fishnish Pier** Ag & B
60 E7 **Fiskavaig** Highld
87 c6 **Fladdabister** Shet
60 E4 **Flashader** Highld
27 H6 **Flemington** S Lans
70 C6 **Flodigarry** Highld
67 H3 **Fochabers** Moray
31 G8 **Fogo** Border
66 F3 **Fogwatt** Moray
80 B5 **Foindle** Highld
47 J4 **Folda** Angus
68 D7 **Folla Rule** Abers
57 H3 **Forbestown** Abers
34 C6 **Ford** Ag & B
29 G2 **Fordell** Fife
49 J2 **Fordoun** Abers
68 B2 **Fordyce** Abers
37 K8 **Forest Mill** Clacks
48 D6 **Forfar** Angus
38 A4 **Forgandenny** P & K
67 J4 **Forgie** Moray
67 J4 **Forgieside** Moray
68 B5 **Forgue** Abers
65 L4 **Fornighty** Highld
66 C3 **Forres** Moray
79 M2 **Forse** Highld
82 C6 **Forsinard** Highld
54 B4 **Fort Augustus** Highld
37 L1 **Forteviot** P & K
28 C7 **Forth** S Lans
46 B6 **Fortingall** P & K
68 C5 **Fortrie** Abers
65 H3 **Fortrose** Highld
43 L2 **Fort William** Highld
46 C5 **Foss** P & K

87 a6 **Foula** Shet
31 J7 **Foulden** Border
29 L8 **Fountainhall** Border
75 H3 **Fourpenny** Highld
59 H2 **Foveran** Abers
38 E2 **Fowlis** Angus
37 J3 **Fowlis Wester** P & K
26 E6 **Foxbar** Rens
54 D2 **Foyers** Highld
65 L4 **Foynesfield** Highld
69 J2 **Fraserburgh** Abers
46 C5 **Frenich** P & K
83 L3 **Freswick** Highld
38 E6 **Freuchie** Fife
40 F5 **Friesland Bay** Ag & B
48 F6 **Friockheim** Angus
20 B4 **Frogden** Border
42 C6 **Fuinary** Highld
15 H2 **Fullarton** N Ayrs
26 E7 **Fullwood** E Ayrs
36 F3 **Funtullich** P & K
34 E7 **Furnace** Ag & B
68 E6 **Fyvie** Abers

G

26 E7 **Gabroc Hill** E Ayrs
15 K5 **Gadgirth** S Ayrs
15 H3 **Gailes** N Ayrs
71 J6 **Gairloch** Highld
53 J8 **Gairlochy** Highld
38 B7 **Gairneybridge** P & K
19 G3 **Galashiels** Border
34 B3 **Gallanach** Ag & B
38 E8 **Gallatown** Fife
54 E7 **Gallovie** Highld
7 J5 **Galloway Forest Park** D & G
48 D7 **Gallowfauld** Angus
38 B1 **Gallowhill** P & K
52 C2 **Galltair** Highld
15 L3 **Galston** E Ayrs
68 F2 **Gamrie** Abers
34 B2 **Ganavan Bay** Ag & B
48 F3 **Gannachy** Angus
67 H4 **Garbity** Moray
57 G4 **Garchory** Abers
68 F2 **Gardenstown** Abers
87 c5 **Garderhouse** Shet
25 L1 **Garelochhead** Ag & B
36 F8 **Gargunnock** Stirlg
3 K5 **Garlieston** D & G
58 E4 **Garlogie** Abers
68 F4 **Garmond** Abers
67 H2 **Garmouth** Moray
27 J5 **Garnkirk** N Lans
84 g2 **Garrabost** W Isls
16 B5 **Garrallan** E Ayrs
7 M6 **Garroch** D & G
2 D7 **Garrochtrie** D & G
25 J7 **Garrochty** Ag & B
61 H2 **Garros** Highld
23 G6 **Gartachossan** Ag & B
27 J5 **Gartcosh** N Lans
27 H5 **Garthamlock** C Glas

67 L7 **Gartly** Abers
36 C7 **Gartmore** Stirlg
27 K5 **Gartness** N Lans
26 F2 **Gartness** Stirlg
26 D2 **Gartocharn** W Duns
79 H5 **Gartymore** Highld
30 D4 **Garvald** E Loth
43 J2 **Garvan** Highld
23 G1 **Garvard** Ag & B
64 B3 **Garve** Highld
33 K5 **Garvellachs** Ag & B
26 B4 **Garvock** Inver
84 f3 **Garyvard** W Isls
15 K3 **Gatehead** E Ayrs
3 M4 **Gatehouse of Fleet** D & G
20 B5 **Gateshaw** Border
48 D7 **Gateside** Angus
26 E6 **Gateside** E Rens
38 C5 **Gateside** Fife
26 C7 **Gateside** N Ayrs
8 F2 **Gateslack** D & G
19 H3 **Gattonside** Border
38 F3 **Gauldry** Fife
47 K6 **Gauldswell** P & K
31 G7 **Gavinton** Border
84 f3 **Gearraidh Bhaird** W Isls
60 D3 **Geary** Highld
47 H8 **Gellyburn** P & K
4 D3 **Gelston** D & G
10 B4 **Georgefield** D & G
83 H4 **Georgemas Junction Station** Highld
86 b5 **Georth** Ork
27 G6 **Giffnock** E Rens
30 C5 **Gifford** E Loth
38 E5 **Giffordtown** Fife
23 L7 **Gigha** Ag & B
30 B5 **Gilchriston** E Loth
60 D3 **Gillen** Highld
9 K4 **Gillesbie** D & G
83 J4 **Gillock** Highld
83 K2 **Gills** Highld
18 E5 **Gilmanscleuch** Border
29 J5 **Gilmerton** C Edin
37 J3 **Gilmerton** P & K
29 L6 **Gilston** Border
15 J2 **Girdle Toll** N Ayrs
87 c5 **Girlsta** Shet
4 A4 **Girthon** D & G
6 E3 **Girvan** S Ayrs
29 M4 **Gladsmuir** E Loth
48 C6 **Glamis** Angus
27 G5 **Glasgow** C Glas
26 E5 *Glasgow Airport* Rens
27 G5 **Glasgow Science Centre** C Glas
51 L6 **Glasnacardoch Bay** Highld
51 H3 **Glasnakille** Highld
27 J8 **Glassford** S Lans
48 F6 **Glasterlaw** Angus
54 D2 **Glebe** Highld
4 B5 **Gledpark** D & G
67 G6 **Glenallachie** Moray
51 K6 **Glenancross** Highld
42 B7 **Glenaros House** Ag & B

13 H3 **Glenbarr** Ag & B
68 B4 **Glenbarry** Abers
42 C4 **Glenbeg** Highld
66 C8 **Glenbeg** Highld
49 J1 **Glenbervie** Abers
27 J5 **Glenboig** N Lans
42 C4 **Glenborrodale** Highld
35 G7 **Glenbranter** Ag & B
17 K5 **Glenbreck** Border
50 F2 **Glenbrittle House** Highld
16 E4 **Glenbuck** E Ayrs
48 B4 **Glencally** Angus
5 H2 **Glencaple** D & G
63 G4 **Glencarron Lodge** Highld
38 C3 **Glencarse** P & K
44 B6 **Glenceitlein** Highld
56 E8 **Glen Clunie Lodge** Abers
43 L5 **Glencoe** Highld
17 L4 **Glencothe** Border
38 C7 **Glencraig** Fife
8 D4 **Glencrosh** D & G
60 B4 **Glendale** Highld
25 G2 **Glendaruel** Ag & B
37 K6 **Glendevon** P & K
54 C4 **Glendoe Lodge** Highld
38 C3 **Glendoick** P & K
38 D4 **Glenduckie** Fife
37 J5 **Gleneagles** P & K
37 J5 **Gleneagles Hotel** P & K
22 F7 **Glenegedale** Ag & B
52 C2 **Glenelg** Highld
66 C5 **Glenerney** Moray
38 B5 **Glenfarg** P & K
55 K6 **Glenfeshie Lodge** Highld
43 H1 **Glenfinnan** Highld
53 K7 **Glenfintaig Lodge** Highld
38 C4 **Glenfoot** P & K
35 H4 **Glenfyne Lodge** Ag & B
26 C7 **Glengarnock** N Ayrs
83 G3 **Glengolly** Highld
41 K5 **Glengorm Castle** Ag & B
61 G5 **Glengrasco** Highld
17 L3 **Glenholm** Border
8 A5 **Glenhoul** D & G
47 K4 **Glenisla** Angus
25 K3 **Glenkin** Ag & B
57 K3 **Glenkindie** Abers
66 F8 **Glenlivet** Moray
4 C3 **Glenlochar** D & G
38 C6 **Glenlomond** P & K
2 E4 **Glenluce** D & G
25 J2 **Glenmassan** Ag & B
27 K5 **Glenmavis** N Lans
61 G6 **Glenmore** Highld
56 B4 **Glenmore Lodge** Highld
44 B3 **Glen Nevis House** Highld
37 H7 **Glenochil** Clacks
48 C4 **Glenquiech** Angus
24 E5 **Glenralloch** Ag & B
38 D7 **Glenrothes** Fife

37 K1 **Glenshee** P & K
54 E6 **Glenshero Lodge** Highld
25 J3 **Glenstriven** Ag & B
55 J6 **Glentromie Lodge** Highld
7 J6 **Glen Trool Lodge** D & G
7 H6 **Glentrool Village** D & G
55 G6 **Glentruim House** Highld
42 D2 **Glenuig** Highld
43 B3 **Glenure** Ag & B
61 G6 **Glenvarragill** Highld
6 E7 **Glenwhilly** D & G
16 F4 **Glespin** S Lans
79 H2 **Glutt Lodge** Highld
34 E7 **Goatfield** Ag & B
29 G4 **Gogar** C Edin
65 J4 **Gollanfield** Highld
75 H2 **Golspie** Highld
87 C4 **Gonfirth** Shet
58 E8 **Goosecruives** Abers
19 K2 **Gordon** Border
18 D4 **Gordon Arms Hotel** Border
68 B3 **Gordonstown** Abers
68 D6 **Gordonstown** Abers
29 K6 **Gorebridge** Mdloth
68 E3 **Gorrachie** Abers
64 B2 **Gorstan** Highld
33 L2 **Gorten** Ag & B
54 E2 **Gorthleck** Highld
68 E6 **Gourdas** Abers
38 F2 **Gourdie** C Dund
49 K3 **Gourdon** Abers
25 L3 **Gourock** Inver
26 F5 **Govan** C Glas
64 D3 **Gower** Highld
28 E1 **Gowkhall** Fife
84 f3 **Grabhair** W Isls
85 c6 **Gramsdal** W Isls
85 c6 **Gramsdale** W Isls
46 E5 **Grandtully** P & K
38 D3 **Grange** P & K
67 K4 **Grange Crossroads** Moray
66 C3 **Grange Hall** Moray
17 J2 **Grangehall** S Lans
28 C3 **Grangemouth** Falk
38 D4 **Grange of Lindores** Fife
28 D3 **Grangepans** Falk
29 H3 **Granton** C Edin
66 C8 **Grantown-on-Spey** Highld
31 G5 **Grantshouse** Border
84 f3 **Gravir** W Isls
25 K6 **Great Cumbrae Island** N Ayrs
28 C6 **Greenburn** W Loth
25 M1 **Greenfield** Ag & B
53 J5 **Greenfield** Highld
27 K4 **Greengairs** N Lans
9 J6 **Greenhill** D & G
27 L3 **Greenhill** Falk
17 H3 **Greenhill** S Lans
16 B3 **Greenholm** E Ayrs

19 H5 **Greenhouse** Border
83 J3 **Greenland** Highld
19 L1 **Greenlaw** Border
9 H6 **Greenlea** D & G
37 H6 **Greenloaning** P & K
26 B3 **Greenock** Inver
17 K2 **Greenshields** S Lans
84 e4 **Greosabhagh** W Isls
60 E4 **Greshornish House Hotel** Highld
10 B8 **Gretna** D & G
10 B8 **Gretna Green** D & G
10 B7 **Gretna Services** D & G
9 J4 **Greyrigg** D & G
48 E7 **Greystone** Angus
15 H7 **Grimmet** S Ayrs
84 f3 **Grimshader** W Isls
84 f3 **Griomaisiader** W Isls
85 c6 **Griomsaigh** W Isls
40 F4 **Grishipoll** Ag & B
86 d6 **Gritley** Ork
85 b7 **Grogarry** W Isls
13 K1 **Grogport** Ag & B
85 b7 **Groigearraidh** W Isls
84 e4 **Grosebay** W Isls
71 L4 **Gruinard** Highld
22 F5 **Gruinart** Ag & B
60 F8 **Grula** Highld
42 B7 **Gruline** Ag & B
87 C5 **Gruting** Shet
44 B7 **Gualachulain** Highld
39 G4 **Guardbridge** Fife
46 F6 **Guay** P & K
38 B2 **Guildtown** P & K
15 J7 **Guiltreehill** S Ayrs
30 B2 **Gullane** E Loth
87 d6 **Gunnista** Shet
87 d2 **Gutcher** Shet
48 F6 **Guthrie** Angus

H

86 C5 **Hackland** Ork
20 B3 **Hadden** Border
30 B4 **Haddington** E Loth
68 F6 **Haddo** Abers
87 C5 **Haggersta** Shet
27 L3 **Haggs** Falk
28 F1 **Halbeath** Fife
83 J4 **Halcro** Highld
83 G4 **Halkirk** Highld
26 D7 **Hall** E Rens
28 B3 **Hall Glen** Falk
60 D3 **Hallin** Highld
18 B2 **Hallyne** Border
27 J7 **Hamilton** S Lans
27 J6 **Hamilton Services** S Lans
87 c6 **Hamnavoe** Shet
80 A6 **Handa Island** Highld
17 G3 **Happendon** S Lans
17 G3 **Happendon Services** S Lans
58 E5 **Hardgate** Abers
4 E2 **Hardgate** D & G
26 F4 **Hardgate** W Duns
19 H5 **Harelaw** Border
10 D6 **Harelaw** D & G

60 D6 **Harlosh** Highld
87 e1 **Haroldswick** Shet
83 G4 **Harpsdale** Highld
51 K2 **Harrapool** Highld
37 K2 **Harrietfield** P & K
84 d4 **Harris** W Isls
28 B5 **Harthill** N Lans
28 B5 **Harthill Services** N Lans
27 L6 **Hartwood** N Lans
18 F4 **Hartwoodmyres** Border
83 K5 **Haster** Highld
69 K6 **Hatton** Abers
48 D7 **Hatton** Angus
58 F3 **Hatton of Fintray** Abers
15 L4 **Haugh** E Ayrs
27 G3 **Haughhead** E Duns
67 J6 **Haugh of Glass** Moray
4 E2 **Haugh of Urr** D & G
19 G6 **Hawick** Border
17 G2 **Hawksland** S Lans
34 F3 **Hayfield** Ag & B
48 E7 **Hayhillock** Angus
17 G1 **Hazelbank** S Lans
38 E3 **Hazelton Walls** Fife
28 B6 **Headlesscross** N Lans
27 J8 **Heads** S Lans
51 K2 **Heast** Highld
9 H6 **Heath Hall** D & G
87 C5 **Heglibister** Shet
19 L4 **Heiton** Border
26 B2 **Helensburgh** Ag & B
15 K3 **Helenton** S Ayrs
79 H5 **Helmsdale** Highld
66 D2 **Hempriggs** Moray
19 L3 **Hendersyde Park** Border
70 B7 **Heribusta** Highld
29 L7 **Heriot** Border
29 G4 **Hermiston** C Edin
10 E3 **Hermitage** Border
6 D5 **Heronsford** S Ayrs
86 c7 **Herston** Ork
86 b5 **Hestwall** Ork
57 J3 **Heughhead** Abers
31 H6 **Heugh Head** Border
40 C7 **Heylipoll** Ag & B
87 C5 **Heylor** Shet
2 C6 **High Ardwell** D & G
8 F5 **High Auldgirth** D & G
27 J6 **High Blantyre** S Lans
27 L3 **High Bonnybridge** Falk
15 K1 **High Cross** E Ayrs
2 D7 **High Drummore** D & G
26 C7 **Highfield** N Ayrs
55 J4 **Highland Wildlife Park** Highld
15 L7 **High Pennyvenie** E Ayrs
9 J6 **Hightae** D & G
28 D2 **High Valleyfield** Fife
28 F2 **Hillend** Fife

37 L7 **Hill End** Fife
29 H5 **Hillend** Mdloth
27 L5 **Hillend** N Lans
68 B7 **Hillhead** Abers
17 J2 **Hillhead** S Lans
69 K5 **Hillhead of**
    Cocklaw Abers
83 H3 **Hilliclay** Highld
26 F5 **Hillington** C Glas
28 F1 **Hill of Beath** Fife
75 H5 **Hill of Fearn** Highld
38 F5 **Hill of Tarvit** Fife
 4 D3 **Hillowton** D & G
59 H5 **Hillside** Abers
49 H4 **Hillside** Angus
87 C3 **Hillswick** Shet
87 C8 **Hillwell** Shet
31 H7 **Hilton** Border
75 J6 **Hilton** Highld
58 D5 **Hirn** Abers
19 J7 **Hobkirk** Border
 9 L7 **Hoddom Cross**
    D & G
 9 K7 **Hoddom Mains**
    D & G
86 e3 **Hollandstoun** Ork
10 A7 **Hollee** D & G
10 C6 **Hollows** D & G
15 K6 **Hollybush** E Ayrs
16 B5 **Holmhead** E Ayrs
27 K6 **Holytown** N Lans
 9 G6 **Holywood** D & G
 9 G6 **Holywood Village**
    D & G
18 D6 **Hopehouse** Border
66 E1 **Hopeman** Moray
31 J8 **Horndean** Border
87 d2 **Horra** Shet
19 H5 **Horsleyhill** Border
18 F6 **Hoscote** Border
37 H3 **Hosh** P & K
87 C7 **Hoswick** Shet
30 D8 **Houndslow** Border
31 H5 **Houndwood**
    Border
65 L4 **Househill** Highld
59 G1 **Housieside** Abers
26 D5 **Houston** Rens
79 K2 **Houstry** Highld
86 b6 **Houton** Ork
83 K3 **Howe** Highld
68 E5 **Howe of Teuchar**
    Abers
 5 L2 **Howes** D & G
29 H6 **Howgate** Mdloth
85 b7 **Howmore** W Isls
20 B5 **Hownam** Border
26 D6 **Howwood** Rens
86 b7 **Hoy** Ork
30 B5 **Humbie** E Loth
19 L2 **Hume** Border
83 L2 **Huna** Highld
19 K5 **Hundalee** Border
25 K3 **Hunter's Quay**
    Ag & B
48 D3 **Hunthill Lodge**
    Angus
30 B4 **Huntington** E Loth
67 L6 **Huntly** Abers
15 L3 **Hurlford** E Ayrs
86 c6 **Hurtiso** Ork
31 J7 **Hutton** Border

17 H2 **Hyndford Bridge**
    S Lans
40 C8 **Hynish** Ag & B

I

60 F2 **Idrigill** Highld
13 L2 **Imachar** N Ayrs
73 K7 **Inchbae Lodge**
    Hotel Highld
48 F4 **Inchbare** Angus
67 G4 **Inchberry** Moray
63 G3 **Incheril** Highld
26 E5 **Inchinnan** Rens
53 J3 **Inchlaggan** Highld
38 D3 **Inchmichael** P & K
54 B3 **Inchnacardoch**
    Hotel Highld
76 F4 **Inchnadamph**
    Highld
38 D2 **Inchture** P & K
63 K6 **Inchvuilt** Highld
38 C4 **Inchyra** P & K
 5 G2 **Ingleston** D & G
69 H6 **Inkhorn** Abers
83 J2 **Inkstack** Highld
25 K4 **Innellan** Ag & B
18 E3 **Innerleithen** Border
38 F7 **Innerleven** Fife
 2 C3 **Innermessan** D & G
30 F4 **Innerwick** E Loth
67 G2 **Innesmill** Moray
68 C8 **Insch** Abers
55 J5 **Insh** Highld
56 F6 **Inver** Abers
75 J5 **Inver** Highld
46 F7 **Inver** P & K
42 F1 **Inverailort** Highld
62 C3 **Inveralligin** Highld
69 K2 **Inverallochy** Abers
74 D2 **Inveran** Highld
34 F5 **Inveraray** Ag & B
61 J7 **Inverarish** Highld
48 D7 **Inverarity** Angus
35 K4 **Inverarnan** Stirlg
71 J4 **Inverasdale** Highld
34 E2 **Inverawe** Ag & B
35 K7 **Inverbeg** Ag & B
49 K2 **Inverbervie** Abers
68 C2 **Inver-boyndie**
    Abers
43 K6 **Invercreran House**
    Hotel Ag & B
55 L3 **Inverdruie** Highld
29 K4 **Inveresk** E Loth
34 E1 **Inveresragan**
    Ag & B
71 K5 **Inverewe Garden**
    Highld
56 D7 **Inverey** Abers
54 D2 **Inverfarigaig**
    Highld
43 J7 **Inverfolla** Ag & B
53 L5 **Invergarry** Highld
36 F7 **Invergeldie** P & K
53 K7 **Invergloy** Highld
74 F7 **Invergordon** Highld
38 F2 **Invergowrie** P & K
52 B4 **Inverguseran**
    Highld
45 L5 **Inverhadden** P & K

35 L3 **Inverherive Hotel**
    Stirlg
52 B5 **Inverie** Highld
34 E4 **Inverinan** Ag & B
52 E2 **Inverinate** Highld
49 G6 **Inverkeilor** Angus
28 F2 **Inverkeithing** Fife
68 C5 **Inverkeithny** Abers
25 L4 **Inverkip** Inver
76 C4 **Inverkirkaig** Highld
72 F4 **Inverlael** Highld
44 E1 **Inverlair** Highld
34 C6 **Inverliever Lodge**
    Ag & B
35 H2 **Inverlochy** Ag & B
48 D1 **Invermark** Angus
67 J6 **Invermarkie** Abers
54 C3 **Invermoriston**
    Highld
81 L4 **Invernaver** Highld
65 G5 **Inverness** Highld
65 J4 *Inverness Dalcross*
    Airport Highld
35 G7 **Invernoaden**
    Ag & B
44 D7 **Inveroran Hotel**
    Ag & B
48 C5 **Inverquharity**
    Angus
69 J5 **Inverquhomery**
    Abers
53 K8 **Inverroy** Highld
43 J4 **Inversanda** Highld
52 E2 **Invershiel** Highld
74 D3 **Invershin** Highld
83 J8 **Invershore** Highld
35 K5 **Inversnaid Hotel**
    Stirlg
69 L5 **Inverugie** Abers
35 K5 **Inveruglas** Ag & B
55 J5 **Inveruglass** Highld
58 E2 **Inverurie** Abers
85 b7 **Iochdar** W Isls
32 D3 **Iona** Ag & B
 8 B6 **Ironmacannie**
    D & G
15 H2 **Irvine** N Ayrs
15 H2 **Irvine Maritime**
    Centre N Ayrs
82 E3 **Isauld** Highld
87 c2 **Isbister** Shet
87 d4 **Isbister** Shet
23 G4 **Islay** Ag & B
22 F7 *Islay Airport* Ag & B
84 f2 **Isle of Lewis** W Isls
33 J1 **Isle of Mull** Ag & B
60 F6 **Isle of Skye** Highld
 3 K7 **Isle of Whithorn**
    D & G
51 L3 **Isleornsay** Highld
 9 G7 **Islesteps** D & G
84 d3 **Islibhig** W Isls
84 d3 **Islivig** W Isls

J

27 G7 **Jackton** S Lans
64 D3 **Jamestown** Highld
26 D3 **Jamestown** W Duns
79 L3 **Janetstown** Highld
83 L5 **Janets-town** Highld

 9 J5 **Jardine Hall** D & G
27 L4 **Jawcraig** Falk
19 K5 **Jedburgh** Border
65 H2 **Jemimaville** Highld
83 L2 **John o' Groats**
    Highld
49 J3 **Johnshaven** Abers
 9 M3 **Johnstone** D & G
26 D5 **Johnstone** Rens
 9 J4 **Johnstonebridge**
    D & G
29 J4 **Joppa** C Edin
15 K5 **Joppa** S Ayrs
29 G5 **Juniper Green**
    C Edin
23 J2 **Jura** Ag & B

K

17 J1 **Kaimend** S Lans
25 G4 **Kames** Ag & B
16 D4 **Kames** E Ayrs
58 B2 **Keig** Abers
37 J8 **Keilarsbrae** Clacks
37 K3 **Keillour** P & K
56 E6 **Keiloch** Abers
23 K5 **Keils** Ag & B
 8 E4 **Keir Mill** D & G
83 L4 **Keiss** Highld
67 J4 **Keith** Moray
47 K8 **Keithick** P & K
48 F4 **Keithock** Angus
64 E3 **Keithtown** Highld
25 L6 **Kelburn** N Ayrs
 5 K2 **Kelhead** D & G
39 G1 **Kellas** Angus
66 E4 **Kellas** Moray
16 E6 **Kelloholm** D & G
19 L3 **Kelso** Border
46 B6 **Keltneyburn** P & K
 9 H7 **Kelton** D & G
38 B8 **Kelty** Fife
39 G4 **Kemback** Fife
58 E3 **Kemnay** Abers
62 B3 **Kenmore** Highld
46 B7 **Kenmore** P & K
24 D5 **Kennacraig** Ag & B
28 C1 **Kennet** Clacks
67 L8 **Kennethmont**
    Abers
38 F6 **Kennoway** Fife
40 C6 **Kenovay** Ag & B
60 F4 **Kensaleyre** Highld
43 K5 **Kentallen** Highld
42 D3 **Kentra** Highld
80 F3 **Keoldale** Highld
52 D1 **Keppoch** Highld
34 B2 **Kerrera** Ag & B
25 J6 **Kerrycroy** Ag & B
84 f3 **Kershader** W Isls
47 K8 **Kettins** P & K
38 E6 **Kettlebridge** Fife
 9 K6 **Kettleholm** D & G
86 d4 **Kettletoft** Ork
 3 J7 **Kidsdale** D & G
43 H8 **Kiel Crofts** Ag & B
23 H5 **Kiells** Ag & B
26 D5 **Kilbarchan** Rens
51 K4 **Kilbeg** Highld
24 C5 **Kilberry** Ag & B
26 C7 **Kilbirnie** N Ayrs

24 C3	**Kilbride** Ag & B
25 H5	**Kilbride** Ag & B
34 B3	**Kilbride** Ag & B
66 D3	**Kilbuiack** Moray
24 D6	**Kilchamaig** Ag & B
25 J7	**Kilchattan** Ag & B
32 E7	**Kilchattan** Ag & B
43 G8	**Kilcheran** Ag & B
41 L4	**Kilchoan** Highld
22 D5	**Kilchoman** Ag & B
34 E3	**Kilchrenan** Ag & B
39 H6	**Kilconquhar** Fife
64 E4	**Kilcoy** Highld
25 L3	**Kilcreggan** Ag & B
13 J5	**Kildalloig** Ag & B
75 G6	**Kildary** Highld
25 G5	**Kildavaig** Ag & B
25 H5	**Kildavanan** Ag & B
79 G4	**Kildonan** Highld
14 D5	**Kildonan** N Ayrs
78 F4	**Kildonan Lodge** Highld
51 G7	**Kildonnan** Highld
2 C4	**Kildrochet House** D & G
57 K2	**Kildrummy** Abers
24 F3	**Kilfinan** Ag & B
53 K6	**Kilfinnan** Highld
6 F2	**Kilgrammie** S Ayrs
40 B7	**Kilkenneth** Ag & B
13 H4	**Kilkenzie** Ag & B
13 J5	**Kilkerran** Ag & B
26 F2	**Killearn** Stirlg
65 G3	**Killen** Highld
45 J5	**Killichonan** P & K
44 D1	**Killiechonate** Highld
42 B7	**Killiechronan** Ag & B
46 E4	**Killiecrankie** P & K
62 E7	**Killilan** Highld
83 K4	**Killimster** Highld
36 C2	**Killin** Stirlg
19 G1	**Killochyett** Border
26 C4	**Kilmacolm** Inver
36 D5	**Kilmahog** Stirlg
34 A8	**Kilmahumaig** Ag & B
70 C6	**Kilmaluag** Highld
38 F3	**Kilmany** Fife
15 K2	**Kilmarnock** E Ayrs
34 B7	**Kilmartin** Ag & B
15 K2	**Kilmaurs** E Ayrs
34 B5	**Kilmelford** Ag & B
13 H5	**Kilmichael** Ag & B
34 B8	**Kilmichael Glassary** Ag & B
24 D2	**Kilmichael of Inverlussa** Ag & B
64 D5	**Kilmorack** Highld
34 C3	**Kilmore** Ag & B
51 K4	**Kilmore** Highld
24 C4	**Kilmory** Ag & B
42 B3	**Kilmory** Highld
14 B5	**Kilmory** N Ayrs
60 D5	**Kilmuir** Highld
65 G4	**Kilmuir** Highld
70 B7	**Kilmuir** Highld
75 G6	**Kilmuir** Highld
25 K3	**Kilmuir** Highld
22 F4	**Kilnave** Ag & B
28 B8	**Kilncadzow** S Lans
34 B3	**Kilninver** Ag & B
32 E7	**Kiloran** Ag & B
14 A4	**Kilpatrick** N Ayrs
39 J6	**Kilrenny** Fife
38 C3	**Kilspindie** P & K
2 D7	**Kilstay** D & G
27 J3	**Kilsyth** N Lans
64 D6	**Kiltarlity** Highld
70 B7	**Kilvaxter** Highld
15 H2	**Kilwinning** N Ayrs
78 F3	**Kinbrace** Highld
37 G6	**Kinbuck** Stirlg
39 G4	**Kincaple** Fife
28 C2	**Kincardine** Fife
74 E4	**Kincardine** Highld
58 B5	**Kincardine O'Neil** Abers
47 J8	**Kinclaven** P & K
59 H5	**Kincorth** C Aber
66 C3	**Kincorth House** Moray
55 K4	**Kincraig** Highld
46 F6	**Kincraigie** P & K
46 F6	**Kindallachan** P & K
24 B7	**Kinerarach** Ag & B
38 C3	**Kinfauns** P & K
25 J6	**Kingarth** Ag & B
59 G5	**Kingcausie** Abers
9 G7	**Kingholm Quay** D & G
29 H2	**Kinghorn** Fife
38 D7	**Kinglassie** Fife
48 B5	**Kingoldrum** Angus
38 E2	**Kingoodie** P & K
39 K5	**Kingsbarns** Fife
60 F4	**Kingsburgh** Highld
14 D4	**Kingscross** N Ayrs
28 F1	**Kingseat** Fife
58 F4	**Kingsford** C Aber
26 E8	**Kingsford** E Ayrs
44 D5	**Kings House Hotel** Highld
36 C4	**Kingshouse Hotel** Stirlg
38 E5	**Kingskettle** Fife
48 D6	**Kingsmuir** Angus
18 C2	**Kings Muir** Border
39 J5	**Kingsmuir** Fife
30 C3	**Kingston** E Loth
67 H2	**Kingston on Spey** Moray
59 G4	**Kingswells** C Aber
55 H5	**Kingussie** Highld
69 H7	**Kinharrachie** Abers
5 G2	**Kinharvie** D & G
37 J4	**Kinkell Bridge** P & K
69 J6	**Kinknockie** Abers
29 G5	**Kinleith** C Edin
50 F5	**Kinloch** Highld
77 H2	**Kinloch** Highld
81 H5	**Kinloch** Highld
47 J7	**Kinloch** P & K
47 L7	**Kinloch** P & K
36 B6	**Kinlochard** Stirlg
80 C4	**Kinlochbervie** Highld
43 J1	**Kinlocheil** Highld
62 F3	**Kinlochewe** Highld
52 E4	**Kinloch Hourn** Highld
54 E7	**Kinlochlaggan** Highld
44 C4	**Kinlochleven** Highld
42 E2	**Kinlochmoidart** Highld
52 B8	**Kinlochnanuagh** Highld
45 L5	**Kinloch Rannoch** P & K
66 C3	**Kinloss** Moray
58 F2	**Kinmuck** Abers
59 G2	**Kinmundy** Abers
12 B2	**Kinnabus** Ag & B
69 H5	**Kinnadie** Abers
46 F5	**Kinnaird** P & K
49 G5	**Kinnaird Castle** Angus
66 F1	**Kinneddar** Moray
49 K2	**Kinneff** Abers
9 H2	**Kinnelhead** D & G
48 F6	**Kinnell** Angus
38 C6	**Kinnesswood** P & K
48 B5	**Kinnordy** Angus
38 B6	**Kinross** P & K
38 C2	**Kinrossie** P & K
38 B6	**Kinross Services** P & K
52 F2	**Kintail** Highld
66 B3	**Kintessack** Moray
38 B4	**Kintillo** P & K
58 E3	**Kintore** Abers
23 H7	**Kintour** Ag & B
22 F8	**Kintra** Ag & B
32 D3	**Kintra** Ag & B
34 B6	**Kintraw** Ag & B
13 J2	**Kintyre** Ag & B
55 L2	**Kinveachy** Highld
36 E7	**Kippen** Stirlg
4 E4	**Kippford or Scaur** D & G
86 b6	**Kirbister** Ork
83 K4	**Kirk** Highld
87 d6	**Kirkabister** Shet
4 A5	**Kirkandrews** D & G
5 G3	**Kirkbean** D & G
48 E7	**Kirkbuddo** Angus
18 D2	**Kirkburn** Border
38 D8	**Kirkcaldy** Fife
4 B5	**Kirkchrist** D & G
2 B2	**Kirkcolm** D & G
16 E6	**Kirkconnel** D & G
4 B3	**Kirkconnell** D & G
5 G2	**Kirkconnell** D & G
3 G3	**Kirkcowan** D & G
4 B5	**Kirkcudbright** D & G
17 G2	**Kirkfieldbank** S Lans
4 F2	**Kirkgunzeon** D & G
64 E5	**Kirkhill** Highld
17 J7	**Kirkhope** S Lans
51 H2	**Kirkibost** Highld
47 L7	**Kirkinch** P & K
3 J5	**Kirkinner** D & G
27 H4	**Kirkintilloch** E Duns
8 E4	**Kirkland** D & G
9 H4	**Kirkland** D & G
16 E6	**Kirkland** D & G
28 F4	**Kirkliston** C Edin
3 K4	**Kirkmabreck** D & G
2 D7	**Kirkmaiden** D & G
47 H4	**Kirkmichael** P & K
15 J7	**Kirkmichael** S Ayrs
16 F2	**Kirkmuirhill** S Lans
28 F5	**Kirknewton** W Loth
67 L7	**Kirkney** Abers
27 L5	**Kirk of Shotts** N Lans
15 G7	**Kirkoswald** S Ayrs
8 F4	**Kirkpatrick** D & G
8 D7	**Kirkpatrick Durham** D & G
10 B7	**Kirkpatrick-Fleming** D & G
67 L7	**Kirkstile** Abers
10 C4	**Kirkstile** D & G
83 L2	**Kirkstyle** Highld
58 C1	**Kirkton** Abers
9 G6	**Kirkton** D & G
38 F3	**Kirkton** Fife
62 C8	**Kirkton** Highld
62 D6	**Kirkton** Highld
37 K4	**Kirkton** P & K
18 C2	**Kirkton Manor** Border
47 L6	**Kirkton of Airlie** Angus
48 B8	**Kirkton of Auchterhouse** Angus
65 K5	**Kirkton of Barevan** Highld
38 C2	**Kirkton of Collace** P & K
57 J3	**Kirkton of Glenbuchat** Abers
69 J7	**Kirkton of Logie Buchan** Abers
48 E4	**Kirkton of Menmuir** Angus
48 E8	**Kirkton of Monikie** Angus
68 D7	**Kirkton of Rayne** Abers
58 F4	**Kirkton of Skene** Abers
38 F1	**Kirkton of Strathmartine** Angus
48 C8	**Kirkton of Tealing** Angus
58 C3	**Kirkton of Tough** Abers
69 J2	**Kirktown** Abers
69 K4	**Kirktown** Abers
68 D3	**Kirktown of Alvah** Abers
58 F1	**Kirktown of Bourtie** Abers
58 F7	**Kirktown of Fetteresso** Abers
67 H6	**Kirktown of Mortlach** Moray
69 K8	**Kirktown of Slains** Abers
17 M1	**Kirkurd** Border
86 C6	**Kirkwall** Ork
86 c6	*Kirkwall Airport* Ork
20 C4	**Kirk Yetholm** Border
25 K3	**Kirn** Ag & B
48 C5	**Kirriemuir** Angus
9 M7	**Kirtlebridge** D & G
81 M3	**Kirtomy** Highld
26 D4	**Kirtonhill** W Duns
3 J4	**Kirwaugh** D & G

62 C6 **Kishorn** Highld
59 H4 **Kittybrewster**
C Aber
69 G5 **Knaven** Abers
51 K4 **Knock** Highld
67 L4 **Knock** Moray
84 g2 **Knock** W Isls
79 K3 **Knockally** Highld
76 F6 **Knockan** Highld
66 F6 **Knockando** Moray
64 E5 **Knockbain** Highld
64 F3 **Knockbain** Highld
25 L5 **Knock Castle** N Ayrs
83 H4 **Knockdee** Highld
25 J4 **Knockdow** Ag & B
7 G3 **Knockeen** S Ayrs
14 D4 **Knockenkelly**
N Ayrs
15 K2 **Knockentiber**
E Ayrs
15 K2 **Knockinlaw** E Ayrs
2 B3 **Knocknain** D & G
23 K4 **Knockrome** Ag & B
7 M5 **Knocksheen** D & G
8 D7 **Knockvennie**
Smithy D & G
7 G7 **Knowe** D & G
8 A4 **Knowehead** D & G
15 G6 **Knoweside** S Ayrs
52 B1 **Kyleakin** Highld
62 B8 **Kyle of Lochalsh**
Highld
52 B2 **Kylerhea** Highld
76 F2 **Kylesku** Highld
52 C6 **Kylesmorar** Highld
84 e4 **Kyles Scalpay** W Isls
76 F2 **Kylestrome** Highld

L

84 f3 **Lacasaigh** W Isls
84 f2 **Lacasdal** W Isls
86 d4 **Lady** Ork
38 E5 **Ladybank** Fife
17 H4 **Ladygill** S Lans
31 J8 **Ladykirk** Border
8 F5 **Lag** D & G
42 D4 **Laga** Highld
12 C1 **Lagavulin** Ag & B
14 B5 **Lagg** N Ayrs
53 L6 **Laggan** Highld
54 F6 **Laggan** Highld
80 F4 **Laid** Highld
71 L3 **Laide** Highld
51 G7 **Laig** Highld
26 E8 **Laigh Clunch** E Ayrs
15 L2 **Laigh Fenwick**
E Ayrs
16 C5 **Laigh Glenmuir**
E Ayrs
27 J7 **Laighstonehall**
S Lans
77 M7 **Lairg** Highld
29 G7 **Lamancha** Border
19 L2 **Lambden** Border
31 K6 **Lamberton** Border
17 J3 **Lamington** S Lans
14 C3 **Lamlash** N Ayrs
17 G2 **Lanark** S Lans
58 E4 **Landerberry** Abers
79 L2 **Land-hallow** Highld

26 D4 **Langbank** Rens
38 E6 **Langdyke** Fife
10 C5 **Langholm** D & G
19 H3 **Langlee** Border
37 G5 **Langside** P & K
79 K4 **Langwell House**
Highld
19 J5 **Lanton** Border
12 C1 **Laphroaig** Ag & B
42 E6 **Larachbeg** Highld
28 B3 **Larbert** Falk
68 B7 **Largie** Abers
24 F2 **Largiemore** Ag & B
39 H5 **Largoward** Fife
25 L6 **Largs** N Ayrs
14 D5 **Largybeg** N Ayrs
14 D4 **Largymore** N Ayrs
25 L4 **Larkfield** Inver
27 K7 **Larkhall** S Lans
38 B8 **Lassodie** Fife
29 J5 **Lasswade** Mdloth
79 L2 **Latheron** Highld
79 L3 **Latheronwheel**
Highld
39 H5 **Lathones** Fife
30 C8 **Lauder** Border
49 H3 **Laurencekirk** Abers
4 B3 **Laurieston** D & G
28 B3 **Laurieston** Falk
27 L7 **Law** S Lans
45 L7 **Lawers** P & K
38 A3 **Lawgrove** P & K
27 L7 **Law Hill** S Lans
84 f3 **Laxay** W Isls
84 f2 **Laxdale** W Isls
80 C6 **Laxford Bridge**
Highld
87 d4 **Laxo** Shet
64 F5 **Leachkin** Highld
29 H7 **Leadburn** Border
17 G6 **Leadhills** S Lans
61 H3 **Lealt** Highld
22 E5 **Lecht Gruinart**
Ag & B
45 L7 **Leckbuie** P & K
72 F4 **Leckmelm** Highld
43 H8 **Ledaig** Ag & B
76 F6 **Ledmore Junction**
Highld
38 C3 **Leetown** P & K
19 J2 **Legerwood** Border
27 H7 **Leigh Knoweglass**
S Lans
47 L7 **Leitfie** P & K
29 H3 **Leith** C Edin
20 B1 **Leitholm** Border
20 B3 **Lempitlaw** Border
84 f3 **Lemreway** W Isls
6 D4 **Lendalfoot** S Ayrs
36 C6 **Lendrick** Stirlg
69 L6 **Lendrum Terrace**
Abers
54 D1 **Lenie** Highld
20 C2 **Lennel** Border
4 A5 **Lennox Plunton**
D & G
27 H3 **Lennoxtown**
E Duns
27 H4 **Lenzie** E Duns
57 L4 **Leochel-Cushnie**
Abers
60 B4 **Lephin** Highld

87 d6 **Lerwick** Shet
58 B1 **Leslie** Abers
38 D6 **Leslie** Fife
16 F2 **Lesmahagow**
S Lans
2 B3 **Leswalt** D & G
48 E6 **Letham** Angus
19 K7 **Letham** Border
28 B2 **Letham** Falk
38 E4 **Letham** Fife
49 G7 **Letham Grange**
Angus
47 H7 **Lethendy** P & K
58 B2 **Lethenty** Abers
68 F6 **Lethenty** Abers
71 L7 **Letterewe** Highld
52 D2 **Letterfearn** Highld
53 K6 **Letterfinlay Lodge**
Hotel Highld
51 M7 **Lettermorar** Highld
72 F4 **Letters** Highld
17 H5 **Lettershaw** S Lans
56 C2 **Lettoch** Highld
66 D7 **Lettoch** Highld
39 G3 **Leuchars** Fife
84 f3 **Leumrabhagh**
W Isls
84 f3 **Leurbost** W Isls
38 F7 **Leven** Fife
87 c7 **Levenwick** Shet
84 d5 **Leverburgh** W Isls
64 D8 **Lewiston** Highld
58 E3 **Leylodge** Abers
69 J4 **Leys** Abers
47 K8 **Leys** P & K
48 F6 **Leysmill** Angus
48 C6 **Leys of Cossans**
Angus
67 G3 **Lhanbryde** Moray
17 J2 **Libberton** S Lans
29 J4 **Liberton** C Edin
42 F4 **Liddesdale** Highld
38 E2 **Liff** Angus
19 H4 **Lilliesleaf** Border
27 J7 **Limekilnburn** S Lans
28 E2 **Limekilns** Fife
28 B4 **Limerigg** Falk
16 C4 **Limmerhaugh**
E Ayrs
9 G6 **Lincluden** D & G
70 B7 **Linicro** Highld
29 J1 **Linktown** Fife
66 F3 **Linkwood** Moray
28 D3 **Linlithgow** W Loth
74 D2 **Linsidemore** Highld
31 H6 **Lintlaw** Border
67 L2 **Lintmill** Moray
20 B4 **Linton** Border
26 E5 **Linwood** Rens
85 b7 **Lionacleit** W Isls
84 g1 **Lional** W Isls
43 G7 **Lismore** Ag & B
3 J5 **Little Airies** D & G
48 F4 **Little Brechin**
Angus
64 F4 **Littleburn** Highld
47 G7 **Little Dunkeld** P & K
4 E3 **Little Knox** D & G
57 H6 **Littlemill** Abers
65 L4 **Littlemill** Highld
64 B3 **Little Scatwell**
Highld

4 C4 **Little Sypland** D & G
48 B6 **Littleton** Angus
4 B4 **Littleton** D & G
84 f3 **Liurbost** W Isls
28 E5 **Livingston** W Loth
28 E5 **Livingston Village**
W Loth
28 C3 **Loan** Falk
29 J5 **Loanhead** Mdloth
5 G4 **Loaningfoot** D & G
15 J3 **Loans** S Ayrs
52 B8 **Lochailort** Highld
42 D7 **Lochaline** Highld
2 C4 **Lochans** D & G
9 H6 **Locharbriggs** D & G
34 D4 **Lochavich** Ag & B
35 G2 **Lochawe** Ag & B
85 c8 **Loch Baghasdail**
W Isls
85 c8 **Lochboisdale** W Isls
33 J3 **Lochbuie** Ag & B
62 D6 **Lochcarron** Highld
33 L2 **Lochdon** Ag & B
33 L2 **Lochdonhead**
Ag & B
24 D3 **Lochead** Ag & B
36 D3 **Lochearnhead**
Stirlg
38 F2 **Lochee** C Dund
43 K2 **Locheilside Station**
Highld
64 F6 **Lochend** Highld
85 c6 **Locheport** W Isls
85 c6 **Loch Euphoirt**
W Isls
8 F7 **Lochfoot** D & G
24 F1 **Lochgair** Ag & B
38 C8 **Lochgelly** Fife
24 E2 **Lochgilphead**
Ag & B
35 H6 **Lochgoilhead**
Ag & B
38 D5 **Lochieheads** Fife
67 G2 **Lochill** Moray
66 B7 **Lochindorb Lodge**
Highld
76 D4 **Lochinver** Highld
35 L8 **Loch Lomond**
Ag & B
63 L2 **Lochluichart** Highld
9 J5 **Lochmaben** D & G
85 c6 **Lochmaddy** W Isls
71 L7 **Loch Maree Hotel**
Highld
85 c6 **Loch nam Madadh**
W Isls
54 E1 **Loch Ness** Highld
38 C7 **Lochore** Fife
24 F7 **Lochranza** N Ayrs
49 H4 **Lochside** Abers
9 G6 **Lochside** D & G
65 J4 **Lochside** Highld
75 J5 **Lochslin** Highld
6 F6 **Lochton** S Ayrs
48 E4 **Lochty** Angus
39 H5 **Lochty** Fife
42 F5 **Lochuisge** Highld
26 C6 **Lochwinnoch** Rens
9 J3 **Lochwood** D & G
9 K5 **Lockerbie** D & G
57 J2 **Logan** E Ayrs
28 C6 **Loganlea** W Loth

49 H4 **Logie** Angus
38 F4 **Logie** Fife
66 C4 **Logie** Moray
57 K4 **Logie Coldstone** Abers
68 C6 **Logie Newton** Abers
49 G4 **Logie Pert** Angus
46 F6 **Logierait** P & K
69 H8 **Logierieve** Abers
61 L4 **Lonbain** Highld
71 K5 **Londubh** Highld
71 J6 **Lonemore** Highld
38 E2 **Longforgan** P & K
30 E6 **Longformacus** Border
69 L6 **Longhaven** Abers
86 b7 **Longhope** Ork
47 L7 **Longleys** P & K
68 E2 **Longmanhill** Abers
66 F3 **Longmorn** Moray
19 J4 **Longnewton** Border
30 B5 **Long Newton** E Loth
29 L3 **Longniddry** E Loth
28 C5 **Longridge** W Loth
27 L4 **Longriggend** N Lans
69 K5 **Longside** Abers
4 C3 **Longwood** D & G
30 C5 **Longyester** E Loth
69 J3 **Lonmay** Abers
60 D5 **Lonmore** Highld
68 B4 **Lootcherbrae** Abers
47 J6 **Lornty** P & K
66 F1 **Lossiemouth** Moray
79 G6 **Lothbeg** Highld
79 G6 **Lothmore** Highld
2 B2 **Low Barbeth** D & G
51 L2 **Lower Breakish** Highld
62 C3 **Lower Diabaig** Highld
74 D4 **Lower Gledfield** Highld
12 A2 **Lower Killeyan** Ag & B
39 G6 **Lower Largo** Fife
26 E2 **Low Gartachorrans** Stirlg
2 B2 **Low Salchrie** D & G
28 D2 **Low Torry** Fife
81 J6 **Loyal Lodge** Highld
85 b9 **Ludag** W Isls
30 B3 **Luffness** E Loth
16 C5 **Lugar** E Ayrs
30 D4 **Luggate Burn** E Loth
27 K4 **Luggiebank** N Lans
26 D7 **Lugton** E Ayrs
61 J8 **Luib** Highld
33 L5 **Luing** Ag & B
27 H4 **Lumloch** E Duns
58 B4 **Lumphanan** Abers
38 C8 **Lumphinnans** Fife
57 K2 **Lumsden** Abers
49 H6 **Lunan** Angus
48 D6 **Lunanhead** Angus
38 A2 **Luncarty** P & K
38 E1 **Lundie** Angus
39 G6 **Lundin Links** Fife
39 G6 **Lundin Mill** Fife

33 L5 **Lunga** Ag & B
87 d4 **Lunna** Shet
35 L8 **Luss** Ag & B
60 D3 **Lusta** Highld
49 G3 **Luthermuir** Abers
38 E4 **Luthrie** Fife
83 J7 **Lybster** Highld
55 J5 **Lynchat** Highld
18 B2 **Lyne** Border
58 E4 **Lyne of Skene** Abers
86 b7 **Lyness** Ork
66 F7 **Lynn of Shenval** Moray
83 K3 **Lyth** Highld
82 F3 **Lythmore** Highld

M

68 D2 **Macduff** Abers
13 J7 **Macharioch** Ag & B
14 A3 **Machrie** N Ayrs
13 G5 **Machrihanish** Ag & B
32 E8 **Machrins** Ag & B
29 L4 **Macmerry** E Loth
37 K3 **Madderty** P & K
28 C3 **Maddiston** Falk
67 H5 **Maggieknockater** Moray
15 G7 **Maidens** S Ayrs
87 d6 **Mail** Shet
87 c5 **Mainland** Ork
87 c5 **Mainland** Shet
48 E4 **Mains of Balhall** Angus
49 G2 **Mains of Balnakettle** Abers
66 D7 **Mains of Dalvey** Highld
49 H2 **Mains of Haulkerton** Abers
67 K8 **Mains of Lesmoir** Abers
5 G4 **Mainsriddle** D & G
61 G2 **Maligar** Highld
51 L6 **Mallaig** Highld
51 L5 **Mallaigvaig** Highld
29 G5 **Malleny Mills** C Edin
84 d5 **Manais** W Isls
53 L5 **Mandally** Highld
31 G7 **Manderston House** Border
84 d5 **Manish** W Isls
40 C7 **Mannel** Ag & B
59 H4 **Mannofield** C Aber
19 K3 **Manorhill** Border
16 C6 **Mansfield** E Ayrs
17 J6 **March** S Lans
14 D3 **Margnaheglish** N Ayrs
3 M5 **Margrie** D & G
58 D4 **Marionburgh** Abers
61 H2 **Marishader** Highld
9 J5 **Marjoriebanks** D & G
38 E6 **Markinch** Fife
30 C3 **Markle** E Loth
86 b5 **Marwick** Ork
64 D4 **Marybank** Highld
64 E3 **Maryburgh** Highld

59 G5 **Maryculter** Abers
31 G6 **Marygold** Border
27 G4 **Maryhill** C Glas
49 H3 **Marykirk** Abers
66 F6 **Marypark** Moray
2 D7 **Maryport** D & G
49 H5 **Maryton** Angus
58 B6 **Marywell** Abers
59 H5 **Marywell** Abers
49 G7 **Marywell** Angus
15 L4 **Mauchline** E Ayrs
69 H5 **Maud** Abers
64 C6 **Mauld** Highld
19 J4 **Maxton** Border
9 G6 **Maxwell Town** D & G
15 H7 **Maybole** S Ayrs
29 K5 **Mayfield** Mdloth
26 F7 **Mearns** E Rens
47 L7 **Meigle** P & K
16 F6 **Meikle Carco** D & G
27 J7 **Meikle Earnock** S Lans
25 H6 **Meikle Kilmory** Ag & B
47 G8 **Meikle Obney** P & K
47 J7 **Meikleour** P & K
68 D7 **Meikle Wartle** Abers
36 F7 **Meldrum** Stirlg
34 B5 **Melfort** Ag & B
48 E5 **Melgund Castle** Angus
71 K3 **Mellon Charles** Highld
71 K3 **Mellon Udrigle** Highld
81 J3 **Melness** Highld
19 H3 **Melrose** Border
86 b7 **Melsetter** Ork
71 H4 **Melvaig** Highld
82 C3 **Melvich** Highld
69 H2 **Memsie** Abers
48 C5 **Memus** Angus
16 F7 **Mennock** D & G
37 H7 **Menstrie** Clacks
52 C7 **Meoble** Highld
60 F7 **Merkadale** Highld
38 F7 **Methil** Fife
38 F7 **Methilhill** Fife
69 G6 **Methlick** Abers
37 L3 **Methven** P & K
83 K2 **Mey** Highld
84 d2 **Miabhig** W Isls
84 d2 **Miavaig** W Isls
69 H2 **Mid Ardlaw** Abers
86 C4 **Midbea** Ork
58 C5 **Mid Beltie** Abers
28 E5 **Mid Calder** W Loth
83 K7 **Mid Clyth** Highld
68 C3 **Mid Culbeuchly** Abers
9 L6 **Middlebie** D & G
46 D3 **Middlebridge** P & K
24 F1 **Middle Kames** Ag & B
19 K2 **Middlethird** Border
40 B7 **Middleton** Ag & B
38 B6 **Middleton** P & K
15 M3 **Middleyard** E Ayrs
19 H4 **Midlem** Border
64 C6 **Mid Mains** Highld
25 H6 **Midpark** Ag & B

81 J4 **Midtown** Highld
87 d3 **Mid Yell** Shet
57 K4 **Migvie** Abers
28 E2 **Milesmark** Fife
69 J5 **Millbreck** Abers
58 F4 **Millbuie** Abers
64 E4 **Millbuie** Highld
15 K4 **Millburn** S Ayrs
74 E7 **Millcraig** Highld
29 J4 **Millerhill** Mdloth
27 H5 **Millerston** C Glas
27 K7 **Millheugh** S Lans
25 G4 **Millhouse** Ag & B
9 K5 **Millhousebridge** D & G
26 D6 **Milliken Park** Rens
37 H4 **Mill of Drummond** P & K
26 D2 **Mill of Haldane** W Duns
25 K7 **Millport** N Ayrs
59 G5 **Milltimber** C Aber
57 G4 **Milltown** Abers
57 K3 **Milltown** Abers
10 C6 **Milltown** D & G
58 C5 **Milltown of Campfield** Abers
67 G6 **Milltown of Edinvillie** Moray
58 C5 **Milltown of Learney** Abers
38 B6 **Milnathort** P & K
27 G4 **Milngavie** E Duns
60 B4 **Milovaig** Highld
2 F4 **Milton** D & G
8 E7 **Milton** D & G
61 L5 **Milton** Highld
64 D7 **Milton** Highld
64 E4 **Milton** Highld
75 G6 **Milton** Highld
83 L5 **Milton** Highld
26 C5 **Milton** Inver
56 E2 **Milton** Moray
67 L2 **Milton** Moray
47 G4 **Milton** P & K
47 H5 **Milton** P & K
36 B6 **Milton** Stirlg
26 D4 **Milton** W Duns
29 H5 **Milton Bridge** Mdloth
36 D1 **Milton Morenish** P & K
58 B5 **Milton of Auchinhove** Abers
38 E7 **Milton of Balgonie** Fife
26 E1 **Milton of Buchanan** Stirlg
27 H3 **Milton of Campsie** E Duns
65 G6 **Milton of Leys** Highld
57 J6 **Milton of Tullich** Abers
34 D7 **Minard** Ag & B
42 D3 **Mingarrypark** Highld
15 J6 **Minishant** S Ayrs
3 J2 **Minnigaff** D & G
68 E3 **Minnonie** Abers
69 J5 **Mintlaw** Abers
19 H5 **Minto** Border

83 K4 **Mireland** Highld
9 G3 **Mitchellslacks** D & G
3 H5 **Mochrum** D & G
9 J2 **Moffat** D & G
51 G3 **Mol-chlach** Highld
27 J4 **Mollinsburn** N Lans
49 J1 **Mondynes** Abers
37 M2 **Moneydie** P & K
8 D4 **Moniaive** D & G
39 H2 **Monifieth** Angus
48 E8 **Monikie** Angus
38 E5 **Monimail** Fife
15 J4 **Monkton** S Ayrs
3 H6 **Monreith** D & G
58 B2 **Montgarrie** Abers
49 H5 **Montrose** Angus
58 D3 **Monymusk** Abers
37 H3 **Monzie** P & K
27 J4 **Moodiesburn** N Lans
38 E4 **Moonzie** Fife
75 G5 **Morangie** Highld
51 L6 **Morar** Highld
20 B4 **Morebattle** Border
72 E3 **Morefield** Highld
36 D1 **Morenish** P & K
30 C4 **Morham** E Loth
29 H4 **Morningside** C Edin
27 L7 **Morningside** N Lans
49 H4 **Morphie** Abers
52 E2 **Morvich** Highld
15 L2 **Moscow** E Ayrs
40 B7 **Moss** Ag & B
57 K2 **Mossat** Abers
87 d4 **Mossbank** Shet
15 K4 **Mossblown** S Ayrs
19 K6 **Mossburnford** Border
8 B7 **Mossdale** D & G
7 K2 **Mossdale** E Ayrs
27 K6 **Mossend** N Lans
10 D3 **Mosspaul Hotel** Border
65 K4 **Moss-side** Highld
67 H3 **Mosstodloch** Moray
3 L5 **Mossyard** D & G
27 K6 **Motherwell** N Lans
46 E4 **Moulin** P & K
74 E7 **Moultavie** Highld
28 F8 **Mountain Cross** Border
64 E3 **Mountgerald House** Highld
29 H6 **Mount Lothian** Mdloth
9 J7 **Mouswald** D & G
20 B5 **Mowhaugh** Border
54 C8 **Moy** Highld
65 J7 **Moy** Highld
52 D2 **Moyle** Highld
13 H2 **Muasdale** Ag & B
59 G6 **Muchalls** Abers
41 K1 **Muck** Highld
27 G3 **Mugdock** Stirlg
61 G6 **Mugeary** Highld
68 D4 **Muirden** Abers
48 F8 **Muirdrum** Angus
68 D5 **Muiresk** Abers
38 E1 **Muirhead** Angus
38 E6 **Muirhead** Fife
27 J4 **Muirhead** N Lans

16 D4 **Muirkirk** E Ayrs
27 J2 **Muirmill** Stirlg
58 B3 **Muir of Fowlis** Abers
66 E3 **Muir of Miltonduff** Moray
64 E4 **Muir of Ord** Highld
47 G8 **Muir of Thorn** P & K
44 B1 **Muirshearlich** Highld
69 J6 **Muirtack** Abers
37 J5 **Muirton** P & K
64 C4 **Muirton Mains** Highld
47 J7 **Muirton of Ardblair** P & K
67 H4 **Mulben** Moray
33 J1 **Mull** Ag & B
65 G4 **Munlochy** Highld
26 B8 **Munnoch** N Ayrs
83 H2 **Murkle** Highld
52 F6 **Murlaggan** Highld
39 G1 **Murroes** Angus
48 D5 **Murthill** Angus
47 H8 **Murthly** P & K
29 K4 **Musselburgh** E Loth
4 C5 **Mutehill** D & G
37 H4 **Muthill** P & K
83 H5 **Mybster** Highld
58 E5 **Myrebird** Abers
11 G3 **Myredykes** Border

N

71 J5 **Naast** Highld
84 d4 **Na Buirgh** W Isls
65 K3 **Nairn** Highld
79 J5 **Navidale House Hotel** Highld
65 J2 **Navity** Highld
87 d5 **Neap** Shet
76 D3 **Nedd** Highld
26 E6 **Neilston** E Rens
17 G1 **Nemphlar** S Lans
19 K2 **Nenthorn** Border
22 E7 **Nereabolls** Ag & B
27 H6 **Nerston** S Lans
19 H2 **Nether Blainslie** Border
68 F3 **Netherbrae** Abers
27 L8 **Netherburn** S Lans
9 K5 **Nethercleuch** D & G
58 F2 **Nether Crimond** Abers
67 H2 **Nether Dallachy** Moray
17 H7 **Nether Fingland** S Lans
48 B7 **Nether Handwick** Angus
17 K6 **Nether Howcleugh** S Lans
69 K5 **Nether Kinmundy** Abers
4 C6 **Netherlaw** D & G
59 G6 **Netherley** Abers
9 H5 **Nethermill** D & G
69 G5 **Nethermuir** Abers
26 F7 **Netherplace** E Rens
48 E5 **Netherton** Angus
27 K7 **Netherton** N Lans

47 J6 **Netherton** P & K
27 G3 **Netherton** Stirlg
83 L1 **Nethertown** Highld
17 L1 **Netherurd** Border
17 G5 **Nether Whitecleuch** S Lans
56 B2 **Nethy Bridge** Highld
5 G2 **New Abbey** D & G
69 G2 **New Aberdour** Abers
47 K6 **New Alyth** P & K
86 e4 **Newark** Ork
27 K6 **Newarthill** N Lans
29 J5 **Newbattle** Mdloth
5 L3 **Newbie** D & G
39 H1 **Newbigging** Angus
47 L7 **Newbigging** Angus
48 C8 **Newbigging** Angus
17 K1 **Newbigging** S Lans
28 F4 **Newbridge** C Edin
9 G6 **Newbridge** D & G
59 J1 **Newburgh** Abers
69 H3 **Newburgh** Abers
38 D4 **Newburgh** Fife
68 F4 **New Byth** Abers
10 E5 **Newcastleton** Border
29 J4 **Newcraighall** C Edin
16 C6 **New Cumnock** E Ayrs
69 G5 **New Deer** Abers
66 F3 **New Elgin** Moray
75 H6 **Newfield** Highld
8 B6 **New Galloway** D & G
39 G3 **New Gilston** Fife
29 H3 **Newhaven** C Edin
27 L6 **Newhouse** N Lans
17 G2 **New Lanark** S Lans
29 K6 **Newlandrig** Mdloth
10 E4 **Newlands** Border
67 G4 **Newlands of Dundurcas** Moray
10 C5 **New Langholm** D & G
69 J4 **New Leeds** Abers
2 E3 **New Luce** D & G
59 G2 **Newmachar** Abers
27 L6 **Newmains** N Lans
84 f2 **Newmarket** W Isls
58 E8 **New Mill** Abers
19 G7 **Newmill** Border
67 K4 **Newmill** Moray
48 C4 **Newmill of Inshewan** Angus
29 H3 **Newmills** C Edin
28 D2 **Newmills** Fife
38 B2 **Newmiln** P & K
16 B2 **Newmilns** E Ayrs
69 G3 **New Pitsligo** Abers
79 K4 **Newport** Highld
39 G2 **Newport-on-Tay** Fife
15 J4 **New Prestwick** S Ayrs
37 J7 **New Sauchie** Clacks
68 D7 **Newseat** Abers
19 H3 **Newstead** Border
27 K6 **New Stevenston** N Lans

34 F7 **Newton** Ag & B
19 J5 **Newton** Border
64 F4 **Newton** Highld
65 H5 **Newton** Highld
65 J2 **Newton** Highld
83 L5 **Newton** Highld
29 J4 **Newton** Mdloth
66 E2 **Newton** Moray
67 H2 **Newton** Moray
17 H3 **Newton** S Lans
27 H6 **Newton** S Lans
28 E3 **Newton** W Loth
84 c5 **Newton Ferry** W Isls
29 J5 **Newtongrange** Mdloth
59 G6 **Newtonhill** Abers
29 J5 **Newtonloan** Mdloth
26 F7 **Newton Mearns** E Rens
48 F4 **Newtonmill** Angus
55 H5 **Newtonmore** Highld
38 B5 **Newton of Balcanquhal** P & K
39 H6 **Newton of Balcormo** Fife
3 J3 **Newton Stewart** D & G
9 K3 **Newton Wamphray** D & G
16 F7 **Newtown** D & G
54 B4 **Newtown** Highld
26 D6 **Newtown of Beltrees** Rens
19 J3 **Newtown St Boswells** Border
16 F2 **New Trows** S Lans
47 L7 **Newtyle** Angus
29 L4 **New Winton** E Loth
34 D5 **Newyork** Ag & B
59 H5 **Nigg** C Aber
75 H6 **Nigg** Highld
19 K4 **Nisbet** Border
31 G7 **Nisbet Hill** Border
26 F6 **Nitshill** C Glas
43 L4 **North Ballachulish** Highld
30 C2 **North Berwick** E Loth
34 C1 **North Connel** Ag & B
70 C6 **North Duntulm** Highld
71 H5 **North Erradale** Highld
59 G4 **Northfield** C Aber
87 e7 **North Haven** Shet
65 G5 **North Kessock** Highld
29 K6 **North Middleton** Mdloth
68 F5 **North Millbrex** Abers
2 C4 **North Milmain** D & G
48 C5 **Northmuir** Angus
28 F3 **North Queensferry** Fife
86 e3 **North Ronaldsay** Ork

86 e3 *North Ronaldsay Airport* Ork
43 H7 **North Shian** Ag & B
27 K1 **North Third** Stirlg
84 d5 **Northton** W Isls
85 b6 **North Uist** W Isls
87 e1 **Norwick** Shet
37 J8 **Norwood** Clacks
62 D8 **Nostie** Highld
83 L3 **Nybster** Highld

O

28 E5 **Oakbank** W Loth
28 D1 **Oakley** Fife
48 D5 **Oathlaw** Angus
34 B2 **Oban** Ag & B
47 G8 **Obney** P & K
83 J7 **Occumster** Highld
15 L5 **Ochiltree** E Ayrs
42 B3 **Ockle** Highld
59 H4 **Old Aberdeen** C Aber
76 D2 **Oldany** Highld
8 D3 **Old Auchenbrack** D & G
4 D2 **Old Bridge of Urr** D & G
6 F3 **Old Dailly** S Ayrs
69 J5 **Old Deer** Abers
30 F4 **Oldhamstocks** E Loth
26 E4 **Old Kilpatrick** W Duns
68 F8 **Oldmeldrum** Abers
68 D8 **Old Rayne** Abers
80 C4 **Oldshoremore** Highld
46 C4 **Old Struan** P & K
83 L5 **Old Wick** Highld
83 G5 **Olgrinmore** Highld
17 L4 **Oliver** Border
87 c3 **Ollaberry** Shet
61 H6 **Ollach** Highld
83 H3 **Olrig House** Highld
43 K4 **Onich** Highld
71 H6 **Opinan** Highld
67 G3 **Orbliston** Moray
60 D5 **Orbost** Highld
68 C3 **Ord** Abers
58 C3 **Ordhead** Abers
57 K5 **Ordie** Abers
67 H3 **Ordiequish** Moray
71 K4 **Ormiscaig** Highld
29 L4 **Ormiston** E Loth
41 L4 **Ormsaigmore** Highld
24 C4 **Ormsary** Ag & B
23 G2 **Oronsay** Ag & B
86 b6 **Orphir** Ork
4 D5 **Orroland** D & G
60 E6 **Ose** Highld
61 H6 **Oskaig** Highld
41 L7 **Oskamull** Ag & B
24 F2 **Otter Ferry** Ag & B
84 c5 **Otternish** W Isls
87 d3 **Otterswick** Shet
77 J4 **Overscaig Hotel** Highld
59 G3 **Overton** C Aber
27 L7 **Overtown** N Lans

19 L5 **Oxnam** Border
30 B7 **Oxton** Border
73 K2 **Oykel Bridge Hotel** Highld
58 D1 **Oyne** Abers

P

84 g2 **Pabail** W Isls
48 C6 **Padanaram** Angus
26 E5 **Paisley** Rens
15 L5 **Palmerston** E Ayrs
4 E4 **Palnackie** D & G
3 J3 **Palnure** D & G
39 J1 **Panbride** Angus
57 J6 **Pannanich Wells Hotel** Abers
86 c3 *Papa Westray Airport* Ork
83 L5 **Papigoe** Highld
30 D4 **Papple** E Loth
8 F4 **Park** D & G
9 H4 **Parkgate** D & G
26 E4 **Parkhall** W Duns
59 G3 **Parkhill House** Abers
27 L6 **Parkside** N Lans
26 F5 **Partick** C Glas
38 E8 **Pathhead** Fife
29 K5 **Pathhead** Mdloth
37 M5 **Path of Condie** P & K
15 K7 **Patna** E Ayrs
31 J7 **Paxton** Border
69 H2 **Peathill** Abers
39 G5 **Peat Inn** Fife
18 C2 **Peebles** Border
61 H7 **Peinchorran** Highld
60 F3 **Peinlich** Highld
29 L5 **Pencaitland** E Loth
29 H6 **Penicuik** Mdloth
61 G6 **Penifiler** Highld
13 J4 **Peninver** Ag & B
6 F3 **Penkill** S Ayrs
68 F2 **Pennan** Abers
33 G3 **Pennycross** Ag & B
33 H3 **Pennyghael** Ag & B
15 H7 **Pennyglen** S Ayrs
8 E4 **Penpont** D & G
13 L1 **Penrioch** N Ayrs
15 J2 **Perceton** N Ayrs
69 H2 **Percyhorner** Abers
38 B3 **Perth** P & K
58 F5 **Peterculter** C Aber
69 L5 **Peterhead** Abers
48 C7 **Petterden** Angus
17 J2 **Pettinain** S Lans
29 H2 **Pettycur** Fife
59 G1 **Pettymuk** Abers
18 F4 **Philiphaugh** Border
28 E3 **Philpstoun** W Loth
55 G6 **Phoines** Highld
58 E3 **Pictillum** Abers
86 c3 **Pierowall** Ork
6 E4 **Pinminnoch** S Ayrs
6 E4 **Pinmore** S Ayrs
6 E5 **Pinwherry** S Ayrs
65 K4 **Piperhill** Highld
19 K4 **Pirnie** Border
13 L1 **Pirnmill** N Ayrs
46 C3 **Pitagowan** P & K

69 J2 **Pitblae** Abers
37 M3 **Pitcairngreen** P & K
75 H6 **Pitcalnie** Highld
58 D1 **Pitcaple** Abers
48 B4 **Pitcarity** Angus
66 E6 **Pitchroy** Moray
30 E4 **Pitcox** E Loth
58 D3 **Pitfichie** Abers
68 D5 **Pitglassie** Abers
75 H3 **Pitgrudy** Highld
48 B4 **Pitkennedy** Angus
38 E5 **Pitlessie** Fife
46 E5 **Pitlochry** P & K
68 C8 **Pitmachie** Abers
55 H5 **Pitmain** Highld
69 G8 **Pitmedden** Abers
69 G8 **Pitmedden Garden** Abers
48 F6 **Pitmuies** Angus
58 C3 **Pitmunie** Abers
38 C3 **Pitroddie** P & K
39 G5 **Pitscottie** Fife
49 H2 **Pittarrow** Abers
39 J6 **Pittenweem** Fife
38 D7 **Pitteuchar** Fife
58 D1 **Pittodrie House Hotel** Abers
69 H2 **Pittulie** Abers
27 L5 **Plains** N Lans
27 L2 **Plean** Stirlg
38 D5 **Pleasance** Fife
62 C7 **Plockton** Highld
76 B6 **Polbain** Highld
28 D5 **Polbeth** W Loth
76 C6 **Polglass** Highld
8 C2 **Polgown** D & G
42 F3 **Polloch** Highld
27 G6 **Pollokshaws** C Glas
27 G5 **Pollokshields** C Glas
28 C3 **Polmont** Falk
52 B8 **Polnish** Highld
34 B7 **Poltalloch** Ag & B
29 J5 **Polton** Mdloth
30 F7 **Polwarth** Border
29 H6 **Pomathorn** Mdloth
71 K5 **Poolewe** Highld
37 L7 **Pool of Muckhart** Clacks
24 C6 **Portachoillan** Ag & B
62 B7 **Port-an-Eorna** Highld
43 H7 **Port Appin** Ag & B
23 H5 **Port Askaig** Ag & B
24 F4 **Portavadie** Ag & B
25 J5 **Port Bannatyne** Ag & B
22 E6 **Port Charlotte** Ag & B
25 G4 **Port Driseach** Ag & B
12 C1 **Port Ellen** Ag & B
58 E2 **Port Elphinstone** Abers
6 B7 **Portencalzie** D & G
25 K8 **Portencross** N Ayrs
67 K2 **Portessie** Moray
26 C4 **Port Glasgow** Inver
67 J2 **Portgordon** Moray
79 H5 **Portgower** Highld
71 H6 **Port Henderson** Highld

35 J8 **Portincaple** Ag & B
34 D5 **Portinnisherrich** Ag & B
67 K2 **Portknockie** Moray
59 H6 **Portlethen** Abers
4 F4 **Portling** D & G
2 D6 **Port Logan** D & G
75 K5 **Portmahomack** Highld
41 K1 **Port Mor** Highld
43 H6 **Portnacroish** Ag & B
84 g2 **Portnaguran** W Isls
22 D7 **Portnahaven** Ag & B
60 E7 **Portnalong** Highld
84 g2 **Port nan Giuran** W Isls
84 c5 **Port nan Long** W Isls
84 c5 **Port nan Long** W Isls
84 g1 **Port Nis** W Isls
29 J4 **Portobello** C Edin
36 D6 **Port of Menteith** Stirlg
84 g1 **Port of Ness** W Isls
2 B4 **Portpatrick** D & G
43 H7 **Port Ramsay** Ag & B
61 G5 **Portree** Highld
82 C3 **Portskerra** Highld
2 B3 **Portslogan** D & G
34 F3 **Portsonachan Hotel** Ag & B
68 B2 **Portsoy** Abers
41 K3 **Portuairk** Highld
22 D7 **Port Wemyss** Ag & B
3 H6 **Port William** D & G
3 K7 **Portyerrock** D & G
18 B3 **Posso** Border
58 B6 **Potarch** Abers
59 H3 **Potterton** Abers
3 K5 **Pouton** D & G
5 K2 **Powfoot** D & G
37 L7 **Powmill** P & K
47 J3 **Presnerb** Angus
31 G6 **Preston** Border
29 K4 **Prestonpans** E Loth
15 J4 **Prestwick** S Ayrs
15 J4 *Prestwick Airport* S Ayrs
16 B2 **Priestland** E Ayrs
31 G6 **Primrosehill** Border
20 B4 **Primsidemill** Border
30 C3 **Prora** E Loth
68 F2 **Protstonhill** Abers
28 E4 **Pumpherston** W Loth

Q

87 c6 **Quarff** Shet
26 C5 **Quarrier's Village** Inver
66 E2 **Quarrywood** Moray
25 L6 **Quarter** N Ayrs
27 J7 **Quarter** S Lans
36 B6 **Queen Elizabeth Forest Park** Stirlg

27 H5 **Queenslie** C Glas
27 J3 **Queenzieburn** N Lans
31 G5 **Quixwood** Border
37 H3 **Quoig** P & K
17 J2 **Quothquan** S Lans
86 c6 **Quoyburray** Ork
86 b5 **Quoyloo** Ork

R

61 J5 **Raasay** Highld
17 L3 **Rachan Mill** Border
9 H7 **Racks** D & G
86 a7 **Rackwick** Ork
65 H3 **Raddery** Highld
39 G5 **Radernie** Fife
66 C3 **Rafford** Moray
65 J8 **Raigbeg** Highld
38 D3 **Rait** P & K
55 H5 **Ralia** Highld
60 B5 **Ramasaig** Highld
79 K3 **Ramscraigs** Highld
26 D5 **Ranfurly** Rens
15 L6 **Rankinston** E Ayrs
45 G5 **Rannoch Station** P & K
37 G7 **Raploch** Stirlg
86 c4 **Rapness** Ork
4 D5 **Rascarrel** D & G
25 K2 **Rashfield** Ag & B
52 E2 **Ratagan** Highld
69 J3 **Rathen** Abers
38 F3 **Rathillet** Fife
28 F4 **Ratho** C Edin
28 F4 **Ratho Station** C Edin
67 K2 **Rathven** Moray
83 J2 **Rattar** Highld
47 J7 **Rattray** P & K
17 H1 **Ravenstruther** S Lans
75 G3 **Rearquhar** Highld
82 D3 **Reay** Highld
65 L5 **Redburn** Highld
4 E2 **Redcastle** D & G
64 E4 **Redcastle** Highld
28 C3 **Redding** Falk
28 C3 **Reddingmuirhead** Falk
49 J3 **Redford** Abers
48 F7 **Redford** Angus
18 E6 **Redfordgreen** Border
38 A2 **Redgorton** P & K
58 E4 **Redhill** Abers
86 b5 **Redland** Ork
49 J2 **Redmyre** Abers
19 J3 **Redpath** Border
71 H7 **Redpoint** Highld
38 C1 **Redstone** P & K
76 B5 **Reiff** Highld
59 G2 **Reisque** Abers
83 L5 **Reiss** Highld
66 B5 **Relugas** Moray
26 F5 **Renfrew** Rens
26 D3 **Renton** W Duns
65 H5 **Resaurie** Highld
42 E4 **Resipole** Highld
65 G2 **Resolis** Highld

35 J6 **Rest and be thankful** Ag & B
31 H6 **Reston** Border
48 E6 **Reswallie** Angus
64 D5 **Rheindown** Highld
76 D4 **Rhicarn** Highld
80 E5 **Rhiconich** Highld
74 F6 **Rhicullen** Highld
72 D3 **Rhireavach** Highld
75 H2 **Rhives** Highld
4 C3 **Rhonehouse** D & G
26 B2 **Rhu** Ag & B
25 H4 **Rhubodach** Ag & B
24 C8 **Rhunahaorine** Ag & B
38 B4 **Rhynd** P & K
67 L8 **Rhynie** Abers
75 J5 **Rhynie** Highld
10 F3 **Riccarton** Border
15 K3 **Riccarton** E Ayrs
19 H4 **Riddell** Border
10 B8 **Rigg** D & G
27 K4 **Riggend** N Lans
65 K4 **Righoul** Highld
17 G3 **Rigside** S Lans
4 C4 **Ringford** D & G
67 G5 **Ringorm** Moray
12 B2 **Risabus** Ag & B
64 E4 **Riverford** Highld
28 B7 **Roadmeetings** S Lans
16 B5 **Roadside** E Ayrs
83 H4 **Roadside** Highld
60 D5 **Roag** Highld
7 G2 **Roan of Craigoch** S Ayrs
18 F6 **Roberton** Border
17 H4 **Roberton** S Lans
9 M7 **Robgill Tower** D & G
4 E4 **Rockcliffe** D & G
75 K5 **Rockfield** Highld
25 L1 **Rockville** Ag & B
84 D5 **Rodel** W Isls
78 C7 **Rogart** Highld
84 d5 **Roghadal** W Isls
29 G8 **Romanno Bridge** Border
60 F4 **Romesdal** Highld
61 K3 **Rona** Highld
24 C7 **Ronachan** Ag & B
69 K4 **Rora** Abers
67 J4 **Rosarie** Moray
27 L1 **Rosebank** S Lans
77 K7 **Rosehall** Highld
69 H2 **Rosehearty** Abers
66 E2 **Roseisle** Moray
65 H3 **Rosemarkie** Highld
47 J7 **Rosemount** P & K
29 J6 **Rosewell** Mdloth
60 D5 **Roskhill** Highld
29 H5 **Roslin** Mdloth
26 B2 **Rosneath** Ag & B
4 B6 **Ross** D & G
26 E4 **Rossland** Rens
83 J7 **Roster** Highld
28 F2 **Rosyth** Fife
67 G4 **Rothes** Moray
25 J5 **Rothesay** Ag & B
68 E6 **Rothiebrisbane** Abers
67 M5 **Rothiemay** Moray

56 B4 **Rothiemurchus Lodge** Highld
68 D7 **Rothienorman** Abers
68 D7 **Rothmaise** Abers
48 B3 **Rottal Lodge** Angus
9 H6 **Roucan** D & G
57 H3 **Roughpark** Abers
48 C6 **Roundyhill** Angus
86 C4 **Rousay** Ork
25 L6 **Routenburn** N Ayrs
10 D6 **Rowanburn** D & G
35 L7 **Rowardennan** Stirlg
19 L4 **Roxburgh** Border
44 D1 **Roy Bridge** Highld
40 D6 **Ruaig** Ag & B
85 c9 **Rubha Ban** W Isls
19 J5 **Ruecastle** Border
50 F5 **Rùm** Highld
67 J4 **Rumbach** Moray
37 L7 **Rumbling Bridge** P & K
28 C3 **Rumford** Falk
47 L3 **Runtaleave** Angus
36 D7 **Ruskie** Stirlg
19 K4 **Rutherford** Border
27 H6 **Rutherglen** S Lans
59 H4 **Ruthrieston** C Aber
67 L5 **Ruthven** Abers
47 L6 **Ruthven** Angus
55 H5 **Ruthven** Highld
5 J2 **Ruthwell** D & G

S

13 K3 **Saddell** Ag & B
31 J5 **St Abbs** Border
30 E5 **St Agnes** Border
39 H4 **St Andrews** Fife
39 H4 **St Andrews Botanic Garden** Fife
9 J4 **St Ann's** D & G
19 J3 **St Boswells** Border
35 G6 **St Catherines** Ag & B
25 H5 **St Colmac** Ag & B
69 K2 **St Combs** Abers
49 J4 **St Cyrus** Abers
37 K4 **St David's** P & K
69 K4 **St Fergus** Abers
36 F3 **St Fillans** P & K
17 J3 **St John's Kirk** S Lans
8 B6 **St John's Town of Dalry** D & G
68 E7 **St Katherines** Abers
38 C3 **St Madoes** P & K
86 C7 **St Margaret's Hope** Ork
38 B2 **St Martin's** P & K
86 c6 **St Mary's** Ork
39 H6 **St Monans** Fife
37 G8 **St Ninians** Stirlg
15 J5 **St Quivox** S Ayrs
49 G7 **St Vigeans** Angus
42 C7 **Salen** Ag & B
42 D4 **Salen** Highld
37 L8 **Saline** Fife
27 L5 **Salsburgh** N Lans
75 G7 **Saltburn** Highld

15 G2 **Saltcoats** N Ayrs
86 d5 **Samsonlane** Ork
30 B4 **Samuelston** E Loth
22 E4 **Sanaigmore** Ag & B
51 L5 **Sandaig** Highld
51 G7 **Sandavore** Highld
86 d4 **Sanday** Ork
86 d4 *Sanday Airport* Ork
25 K3 **Sandbank** Ag & B
68 B2 **Sandend** Abers
16 E2 **Sandford** S Lans
69 H2 **Sandhaven** Abers
2 D5 **Sandhead** D & G
34 E7 **Sandhole** Ag & B
87 b5 **Sandness** Shet
87 c7 **Sandwick** Shet
84 g2 **Sandwick** W Isls
9 L4 **Sandyford** D & G
4 F4 **Sandyhills** D & G
80 F3 **Sangobeg** Highld
80 F3 **Sangomore** Highld
41 K3 **Sanna Bay** Highld
84 g2 **Sanndabhaig** W Isls
14 C1 **Sannox** N Ayrs
16 F7 **Sanquhar** D & G
83 L6 **Sarclet** Highld
58 D3 **Sauchen** Abers
38 C2 **Saucher** P & K
49 G3 **Sauchieburn** Abers
32 E8 **Scalasaig** Ag & B
87 C6 **Scalloway** Shet
61 J7 **Scalpay** Highld
43 G2 **Scamodale** Highld
64 F6 **Scaniport** Highld
33 K6 **Scarba** Ag & B
83 J2 **Scarfskerry** Highld
40 D7 **Scarinish** Ag & B
87 c4 *Scatsta Airport* Shet
38 B3 **Scone** P & K
61 H7 **Sconser** Highld
38 F6 **Scoonie** Fife
72 C3 **Scoraig** Highld
38 C6 **Scotlandwell** P & K
83 G4 **Scotscalder Station** Highld
58 B2 **Scotsmill** Abers
26 F5 **Scotstoun** C Glas
80 B6 **Scourie** Highld
80 B6 **Scourie More** Highld
87 c7 **Scousburgh** Shet
83 G2 **Scrabster** Highld
19 K5 **Scraesburgh** Border
47 K5 **Scruschloch** Angus
81 J4 **Scullomie** Highld
61 G5 **Seafield** Highld
28 D5 **Seafield** W Loth
25 L8 **Seamill** N Ayrs
19 G4 **Selkirk** Border
87 d2 **Sellafirth** Shet
29 L4 **Seton Mains** E Loth
84 g1 **Sgiogarstaigh** W Isls
84 f1 **Shader** W Isls
48 D4 **Shandford** Angus
26 B2 **Shandon** Ag & B
75 J6 **Shandwick** Highld
86 c5 **Shapinsay** Ork
84 e2 **Shawbost** W Isls
8 F6 **Shawhead** D & G
27 K7 **Shawsburn** S Lans
5 H2 **Shearington** D & G

82 E3 **Shebster** Highld
27 G6 **Sheddens** E Rens
80 B4 **Sheigra** Highld
3 H3 **Shennanton** D & G
27 H5 **Shettleston** C Glas
52 E2 **Shiel Bridge** Highld
62 C4 **Shieldaig** Highld
9 H5 **Shieldhill** D & G
28 B3 **Shieldhill** Falk
17 J2 **Shieldhill House Hotel** S Lans
27 K7 **Shields** N Lans
42 D3 **Shielfoot** Highld
48 C5 **Shielhill** Angus
25 L4 **Shielhill** Inver
26 E6 **Shillford** E Rens
77 L5 **Shinness** Highld
24 E2 **Shirvan** Ag & B
14 B4 **Shiskine** N Ayrs
15 K3 **Shortlees** E Ayrs
28 B6 **Shotts** N Lans
66 F4 **Shougle** Moray
33 M5 **Shuna** Ag & B
82 F4 **Shurrery** Highld
82 F4 **Shurrery Lodge** Highld
84 e2 **Siabost** W Isls
84 f1 **Siadar** W Isls
83 K5 **Sibster** Highld
29 G6 **Silverburn** Mdloth
68 E2 **Silverford** Abers
20 C1 **Simprim** Border
31 G7 **Sinclair's Hill** Border
15 L6 **Sinclairston** E Ayrs
57 K3 **Sinnarhard** Abers
86 d6 **Skaill** Ork
16 B6 **Skares** E Ayrs
59 G6 **Skateraw** Abers
30 F4 **Skateraw** E Loth
60 F5 **Skeabost** Highld
75 H3 **Skelbo** Highld
75 H3 **Skelbo Street** Highld
25 L5 **Skelmorlie** N Ayrs
81 L4 **Skelpick** Highld
8 E5 **Skelston** D & G
58 E4 **Skene House** Abers
81 K3 **Skerray** Highld
80 C5 **Skerricha** Highld
82 E3 **Skiall** Highld
84 g1 **Skigersta** W Isls
28 B2 **Skinflats** Falk
60 C5 **Skinidin** Highld
24 F6 **Skipness** Ag & B
10 C5 **Skipper's Bridge** D & G
17 L2 **Skirling** Border
83 L2 **Skirza** Highld
51 K2 **Skulamus** Highld
56 B1 **Skye of Curr** Highld
68 F5 **Slacks of Cairnbanno** Abers
28 B4 **Slamannan** Falk
74 E3 **Sleasdairidh** Highld
83 K3 **Slickly** Highld
14 B5 **Sliddery** N Ayrs
61 G7 **Sligachan** Highld
25 K1 **Sligrachan** Ag & B
34 B7 **Slockavullin** Ag & B
4 B2 **Slogarie** D & G
62 D6 **Slumbay** Highld
19 K3 **Smailholm** Border

42 D2 **Smearisary** Highld
79 L2 **Smerral** Highld
71 J6 **Smithstown** Highld
65 H5 **Smithton** Highld
80 F3 **Smoo** Highld
8 E5 **Snade** D & G
51 G3 **Soay** Highld
84 c5 **Solas** W Isls
10 B6 **Solwaybank** D & G
3 J5 **Sorbie** D & G
83 G3 **Sordale** Highld
41 H4 **Sorisdale** Ag & B
16 B4 **Sorn** E Ayrs
83 K3 **Sortat** Highld
67 H4 **Sound Muir** Moray
37 J8 **South Alloa** Falk
43 L5 **South Ballachulish** Highld
13 H7 **Southend** Ag & B
5 G4 **Southerness** D & G
71 H7 **South Erradale** Highld
27 L4 **Southfield** Falk
29 G4 **South Gyle** C Edin
65 G5 **South Kessock** Highld
48 C5 **Southmuir** Angus
28 F3 **South Queensferry** C Edin
86 c7 **South Ronaldsay** Ork
43 H7 **South Shian** Ag & B
28 D7 **South Tarbrax** S Lans
85 c8 **South Uist** W Isls
53 K8 **Spean Bridge** Highld
67 H2 **Spey Bay** Moray
56 C1 **Speybridge** Highld
67 G6 **Speyview** Moray
74 F4 **Spinningdale** Highld
30 B3 **Spittal** E Loth
83 H5 **Spittal** Highld
47 H7 **Spittalfield** P & K
57 G7 **Spittal of Glenmuick** Abers
47 H3 **Spittal of Glenshee** P & K
19 J5 **Spittal-on-Rule** Border
30 E4 **Spott** E Loth
30 D7 **Spottiswoode** Border
27 G5 **Springburn** C Glas
10 B7 **Springfield** D & G
38 E5 **Springfield** Fife
8 E7 **Springholm** D & G
15 J2 **Springside** N Ayrs
20 A3 **Sprouston** Border
85 b7 **Stadhlaigearraidh** W Isls
70 D7 **Staffin** Highld
15 K5 **Stair** E Ayrs
2 E4 **Stairhaven** D & G
27 K5 **Stand** N Lans
28 C4 **Standburn** Falk
28 B6 **Stane** N Lans
17 L4 **Stanhope** Border
38 B2 **Stanley** P & K
85 b8 **Staoinebrig** W Isls
38 E6 **Star** Fife

83 L5 **Staxigoe** Highld
37 L8 **Steelend** Fife
10 F4 **Steele Road** Border
60 D7 **Stein** Highld
8 D4 **Stenhouse** D & G
28 B2 **Stenhousemuir** Falk
70 D7 **Stenscholl** Highld
30 D4 **Stenton** E Loth
84 f2 **Steornabhagh** W Isls
27 H5 **Stepps** N Lans
15 H2 **Stevenston** N Ayrs
27 H7 **Stewartfield** S Lans
15 K1 **Stewarton** E Ayrs
19 L2 **Stichill** Border
85 b7 **Stilligarry** W Isls
69 L6 **Stirling** Abers
37 G8 **Stirling** Stirlg
27 L2 **Stirling Services** Stirlg
18 B2 **Stobo** Border
19 G7 **Stobs Castle** Border
16 F3 **Stockbriggs** S Lans
76 C3 **Stoer** Highld
24 E4 **Stonefield Castle Hotel** Ag & B
59 G7 **Stonehaven** Abers
27 K8 **Stonehouse** S Lans
67 G2 **Stonewells** Moray
85 b8 **Stoneybridge** W Isls
28 D5 **Stoneyburn** W Loth
2 C4 **Stoneykirk** D & G
59 G3 **Stoneywood** C Aber
27 L2 **Stoneywood** Falk
84 f2 **Stornoway** W Isls
84 g2 *Stornoway Airport* W Isls
66 F1 **Stotfield** Moray
87 C7 **Stove** Shet
19 G1 **Stow** Border
56 B3 **Straanruie** Highld
49 G4 **Stracathro Hospital** Angus
58 D6 **Strachan** Abers
34 F6 **Strachur** Ag & B
29 H5 **Straiton** Mdloth
7 H2 **Straiton** S Ayrs
59 G2 **Straloch** Abers
47 G4 **Straloch** P & K
2 C3 **Stranraer** D & G
71 J5 **Strath** Highld
76 C3 **Strathan** Highld
81 J3 **Strathan** Highld
16 D1 **Strathaven** S Lans
27 G3 **Strathblane** Stirlg
72 F2 **Strathcanaird** Highld
62 E6 **Strathcarron** Highld
33 K2 **Strathcoil** Ag & B
57 H3 **Strathdon** Abers
39 G4 **Strathkinness** Fife
28 C4 **Strathloanhead** W Loth
54 F6 **Strathmashie House** Highld
38 C5 **Strathmiglo** Fife
64 D3 **Strathpeffer** Highld
46 E5 **Strathtay** P & K
14 D3 **Strathwhillan** N Ayrs

82 B3 **Strathy** Highld
82 B3 **Strathy Inn** Highld
36 C4 **Strathyre** Stirlg
39 J5 **Stravithie** Fife
38 C1 **Strelitz** P & K
69 H4 **Strichen** Abers
83 L1 **Stroma** Highld
62 D7 **Stromeferry** Highld
86 b6 **Stromness** Ork
35 L5 **Stronachlachar** Stirlg
25 H3 **Stronafian** Ag & B
76 F5 **Stronchrubie** Highld
25 L3 **Strone** Ag & B
44 B1 **Strone** Highld
53 J8 **Stronenaba** Highld
35 G2 **Stronmilchan** Ag & B
86 d5 **Stronsay** Ork
86 d5 *Stronsay Airport* Ork
43 G4 **Strontian** Highld
60 E6 **Struan** Highld
46 C4 **Struan** P & K
27 K7 **Strutherhill** S Lans
38 F5 **Struthers** Fife
64 B6 **Struy** Highld
69 H5 **Stuartfield** Abers
67 H3 **Stynie** Moray
35 K6 **Succoth** Ag & B
51 J3 **Suisnish** Highld
87 C4 **Sullom** Shet
87 C4 **Sullom Voe** Shet
87 c8 *Sumburgh Airport* Shet
8 E5 **Sundaywell** D & G
22 E5 **Sunderland** Ag & B
18 E4 **Sundhope** Border
37 G7 **Sunnylaw** Stirlg
79 M2 **Swiney** Highld
31 H8 **Swinton** Border
64 E2 **Swordale** Highld
52 B6 **Swordland** Highld
81 M3 **Swordly** Highld
87 d4 **Symbister** Shet
15 J3 **Symington** S Ayrs
17 J3 **Symington** S Lans
81 L6 **Syre** Highld

T

75 G5 **Tain** Highld
83 J3 **Tain** Highld
84 e4 **Tairbeart** W Isls
60 E7 **Talisker** Highld
71 L7 **Talladale** Highld
17 M5 **Talla Linnfoots** Border
7 J3 **Tallaminnock** S Ayrs
81 J3 **Talmine** Highld
85 b9 **Tangusdale** W Isls
86 c6 **Tankerness** Ork
83 K6 **Tannach** Highld
58 E8 **Tannachie** Abers
48 D5 **Tannadice** Angus
27 J6 **Tannochside** N Lans
84 d5 **Taobh Tuath** W Isls
24 B7 **Tarbert** Ag & B
24 E5 **Tarbert** Ag & B
84 e4 **Tarbert** W Isls

35 K6 **Tarbet** Ag & B
52 B6 **Tarbet** Highld
80 B5 **Tarbet** Highld
15 K4 **Tarbolton** S Ayrs
28 D7 **Tarbrax** S Lans
48 D1 **Tarfside** Angus
57 K4 **Tarland** Abers
51 J4 **Tarskavaig** Highld
69 G7 **Tarves** Abers
67 J4 **Tauchers** Moray
34 F3 **Taychreggan Hotel** Ag & B
46 C4 **Tay Forest Park** P & K
13 H1 **Tayinloan** Ag & B
34 E2 **Taynuilt** Ag & B
39 G2 **Tayport** Fife
24 C2 **Tayvallich** Ag & B
51 K4 **Teangue** Highld
64 F2 **Teanord** Highld
18 F7 **Teindside** Border
45 L5 **Tempar** P & K
9 J5 **Templand** D & G
29 J6 **Temple** Mdloth
49 K1 **Temple of Fiddes** Abers
64 E7 **Temple Pier** Highld
9 G6 **Terregles** D & G
10 D2 **Teviothead** Highld
17 J2 **Thankerton** S Lans
61 H7 **The Braes** Highld
30 E4 **The Brunt** E Loth
26 C7 **The Den** N Ayrs
67 G2 **The Lochs** Moray
27 H7 **The Murray** S Lans
58 D5 **The Neuk** Abers
37 G3 **The Ross** P & K
30 C8 **Thirlestane** Border
68 B6 **Thomastown** Abers
8 F3 **Thornhill** D & G
36 E7 **Thornhill** Stirlg
26 F6 **Thornliebank** E Rens
48 C6 **Thornton** Angus
38 E7 **Thornton** Fife
27 G7 **Thorntonhall** S Lans
30 F4 **Thorntonloch** E Loth
30 D8 **Thornydykes** Border
15 J7 **Threave** S Ayrs
4 C3 *Threave Castle* D & G
28 E3 **Three Miletown** W Loth
19 H2 **Threepwood** Border
28 B1 **Throsk** Stirlg
8 F5 **Throughgate** D & G
83 L6 **Thrumster** Highld
83 G2 **Thurso** Highld
37 L3 **Tibbermore** P & K
8 E3 **Tibbers** D & G
18 C5 **Tibbie Shiels Inn** Border
48 E4 **Tigerton** Angus
85 b6 **Tigh a Ghearraidh** W Isls
85 b6 **Tigharry** W Isls
25 G4 **Tighnabruaich** Ag & B
37 J7 **Tillicoultry** Clacks

16 F1 **Tillietudlem** S Lans
58 D4 **Tillybirloch** Abers
58 C3 **Tillyfourie** Abers
59 G2 **Tillygreig** Abers
38 B6 **Tillyrie** P & K
10 B7 **Timpanheck** D & G
84 d2 **Timsgarry** W Isls
84 d2 **Timsgearraidh** W Isls
87 c6 *Tingwall Airport* Shet
9 H5 **Tinwald** D & G
40 D7 **Tiree** Ag & B
40 C7 *Tiree Airport* Ag & B
24 C6 **Tiretigan** Ag & B
87 c8 **Toab** Shet
41 L5 **Tobermory** Ag & B
33 L5 **Toberonochy** Ag & B
85 b7 **Tobha Mor** W Isls
68 D7 **Tocher** Abers
67 L2 **Tochieneal** Moray
48 C8 **Todhills** Angus
87 c3 **Toft** Shet
51 J3 **Tokavaig** Highld
84 g2 **Tolastadh** W Isls
84 g2 **Tolsta** W Isls
65 J8 **Tomatin** Highld
53 K3 **Tomchrasky** Highld
53 H5 **Tomdoun** Highld
63 L8 **Tomich** Highld
64 E5 **Tomich** Highld
74 F7 **Tomich** Highld
78 A7 **Tomich** Highld
56 E2 **Tomintoul** Moray
64 D6 **Tomnacross** Highld
56 F1 **Tomnavoulin** Moray
4 C4 **Tongland** D & G
81 J4 **Tongue** Highld
14 A4 **Torbeg** N Ayrs
75 G2 **Torboll** Highld
65 G6 **Torbreck** Highld
44 B2 **Torcastle** Highld
64 F4 **Tore** Highld
24 D5 **Torinturk** Ag & B
13 M3 **Tormore** N Ayrs
65 J4 **Tornagrain** Highld
58 C4 **Tornaveen** Abers
64 E8 **Torness** Highld
33 L1 **Torosay Castle** Ag & B
28 C4 **Torphichen** W Loth
58 C5 **Torphins** Abers
29 L8 **Torquhan** Border
61 J5 **Torran** Highld
27 H4 **Torrance** E Duns
15 J1 **Torranyard** N Ayrs
62 D3 **Torridon** Highld
62 D3 **Torridon House** Highld
51 J2 **Torrin** Highld
13 K3 **Torrisdale** Ag & B
81 K3 **Torrisdale** Highld
79 G5 **Torrish** Highld
78 A7 **Torrobull** Highld
59 H4 **Torry** C Aber
28 D2 **Torryburn** Fife
9 H6 **Torthorwald** D & G
61 H5 **Torvaig** Highld
27 L2 **Torwood** Falk
19 G2 **Torwoodlee** Border
61 L6 **Toscaig** Highld

60 C4 **Totaig** Highld
60 F5 **Tote** Highld
61 H3 **Tote** Highld
40 F5 **Totronald** Ag & B
60 F2 **Totscore** Highld
75 J5 **Toulvaddie** Highld
25 K5 **Toward** Ag & B
25 J5 **Toward Quay** Ag & B
57 K4 **Towie** Abers
26 D3 **Townend** W Duns
9 H4 **Townhead** D & G
4 C3 **Townhead of Greenlaw** D & G
28 F1 **Townhill** Fife
20 B4 **Town Yetholm** Border
15 K5 **Trabboch** E Ayrs
15 L5 **Trabbochburn** E Ayrs
65 K3 **Tradespark** Highld
29 L4 **Tranent** E Loth
82 C5 **Trantelbeg** Highld
82 C5 **Trantlemore** Highld
30 D4 **Traprain** E Loth
18 E3 **Traquair** Border
60 F4 **Treaslane** Highld
41 G7 **Treshnish Isles** Ag & B
46 C4 **Tressait** P & K
87 C5 **Tresta** Shet
87 e3 **Tresta** Shet
46 B4 **Trinafour** P & K
48 F4 **Trinity** Angus
37 K4 **Trinity Gask** P & K
43 L2 **Trislaig** Highld
46 F7 **Trochry** P & K
15 H3 **Troon** S Ayrs
36 B5 **Trossachs** Stirlg
36 B6 **Trossachs Pier** Stirlg
60 C3 **Trumpan** Highld
37 H7 **Tullibody** Clacks
64 F8 **Tullich** Highld
75 J6 **Tullich** Highld
46 F5 **Tulliemet** P & K
68 F7 **Tulloch** Abers
34 D7 **Tullochgorm** Ag & B
44 F1 **Tulloch Station** Highld
37 L1 **Tullybeagles Lodge** P & K
47 J5 **Tullymurdoch** P & K
58 B2 **Tullynessle** Abers
46 B5 **Tummel Bridge** P & K
9 J5 **Tundergarth** D & G
6 E2 **Turnberry** S Ayrs
29 G4 **Turnhouse** C Edin
68 D4 **Turriff** Abers
18 D5 **Tushielaw Inn** Border
86 b5 **Twatt** Ork
87 c5 **Twatt** Shet
27 J3 **Twechar** E Duns
19 H3 **Tweedbank** Border
17 L4 **Tweedsmuir** Border
4 B4 **Twynholm** D & G

35 K2 **Tyndrum** Stirlg
30 D3 **Tyninghame** E Loth
8 E4 **Tynron** D & G

U

27 J6 **Uddingston** S Lans
17 G3 **Uddingston** S Lans
59 G1 **Udny Green** Abers
59 G1 **Udny Station** Abers
13 K4 **Ugadale** Ag & B
85 c8 **Uibhist A Deas** W Isls
85 b6 **Uibhist A Tuath** W Isls
40 F5 **Uig** Ag & B
60 C4 **Uig** Highld
60 F2 **Uig** Highld
84 d2 **Uig** W Isls
61 G5 **Uigshader** Highld
32 E4 **Uisken** Ag & B
83 K7 **Ulbster** Highld
72 E3 **Ullapool** Highld
60 E6 **Ullinish Lodge Hotel** Highld
87 d3 **Ulsta** Shet
41 K7 **Ulva** Ag & B
16 F7 **Ulzieside** D & G
76 F2 **Unapool** Highld
10 E5 **Under Burnmouth** Border
87 d1 **Unst** Shet
28 E4 **Uphall** W Loth
26 E7 **Uplawmoor** E Rens
74 E4 **Upper Ardchronie** Highld
82 C4 **Upper Bighouse** Highld
51 L2 **Upper Breakish** Highld
67 H2 **Upper Dallachy** Moray
82 E3 **Upper Dounreay** Highld
36 E6 **Upper Drumbane** Stirlg
65 J2 **Upper Eathie** Highld
60 E4 **Upperglen** Highld
35 G2 **Upper Kinchrackine** Ag & B
39 G6 **Upper Largo** Fife
58 D6 **Upper Lochton** Abers
83 J7 **Upper Lybster** Highld
67 H4 **Upper Mulben** Moray
3 L3 **Upper Ruscoe** D & G
25 L5 **Upper Skelmorlie** N Ayrs
8 E5 **Upper Stepford** D & G
83 L1 **Uppertown** Highld
39 J1 **Upper Victoria** Angus
20 C1 **Upsettlington** Border
67 G2 **Urquhart** Moray

64 D4 **Urray** Highld
49 H5 **Usan** Angus
87 d2 **Uyeasound** Shet

V

61 H2 **Valtos** Highld
84 d2 **Valtos** W Isls
87 d3 **Vatsetter** Shet
60 D5 **Vatten** Highld
87 c6 **Veensgarth** Shet
87 d4 **Vidlin** Shet
67 C2 **Viewfield** Moray
27 J6 **Viewpark** N Lans
87 c4 **Voe** Shet

W

4 D2 **Walbutt** D & G
18 E3 **Walkerburn** Border
38 D6 **Walkerton** Fife
7 G2 **Wallacetown** S Ayrs
15 J5 **Wallacetown** S Ayrs
87 b5 **Walls** Shet
29 K4 **Wallyford** E Loth
17 K1 **Walston** S Lans
17 G6 **Wanlockhead** D & G
5 L2 **Warmanbie** D & G
17 J2 **Warrenhill** S Lans
29 H4 **Warriston** C Edin
86 c4 **Wasbister** Ork
9 M6 **Waterbeck** D & G
27 G7 **Waterfoot** E Rens
29 H7 **Waterheads** Border
51 K2 **Waterloo** Highld
27 L7 **Waterloo** N Lans
47 G8 **Waterloo** P & K
15 K7 **Waterside** E Ayrs
15 L2 **Waterside** E Ayrs
27 J4 **Waterside** E Duns
60 B5 **Waterstein** Highld
83 J5 **Watten** Highld
27 K4 **Wattston** N Lans
58 C6 **Waulkmill** Abers
68 F7 **Wedderlairs** Abers

46 D6 **Weem** P & K
87 c5 **Weisdale** Shet
48 D8 **Wellbank** Angus
37 K3 **Welltree** P & K
28 E2 **Wellwood** Fife
25 L4 **Wemyss Bay** Inver
30 E3 **West Barns** E Loth
2 D8 **West Cairngaan** D & G
28 D5 **West Calder** W Loth
83 J2 **West Dunnet** Highld
83 G5 **Westerdale** Highld
64 F7 **Wester Drumashie** Highld
28 D4 **Wester Ochiltree** W Loth
39 J6 **Wester Pitkierie** Fife
72 C5 **Wester Ross** Highld
49 G5 **Westerton** Angus
87 c6 **Westerwick** Shet
82 F3 **Westfield** Highld
27 J4 **Westfield** N Lans
28 C4 **Westfield** W Loth
47 J6 **Westfields of Rattray** P & K
39 J1 **West Haven** Angus
79 H5 **West Helmsdale** Highld
58 F4 **Westhill** Abers
37 M3 **West Huntingtower** P & K
25 L8 **West Kilbride** N Ayrs
43 L5 **West Laroch** Highld
28 F7 **West Linton** Border
19 J2 **West Morriston** Border
48 B5 **Westmuir** Angus
58 E5 **West Park** Abers
28 B3 **Westquarter** Falk
86 c3 **Westray** Ork
86 c3 *Westray Airport* Ork
28 B5 **Westrigg** W Loth
30 D7 **Westruther** Border

30 B5 **West Saltoun** E Loth
87 d3 **West Sandwick** Shet
24 E5 **West Tarbert** Ag & B
38 E7 **West Wemyss** Fife
83 H3 **Weydale** Highld
83 K7 **Whaligoe** Highld
87 d4 **Whalsay** Shet
3 J5 **Whauphill** D & G
48 D7 **Whigstreet** Angus
4 C4 **Whinnie Liggate** D & G
69 K7 **Whinnyfold** Abers
35 J8 **Whistlefield** Ag & B
35 G8 **Whistlefield Inn** Ag & B
28 C5 **Whitburn** W Loth
30 F6 **Whitchester** Border
54 D3 **Whitebridge** Highld
59 H2 **Whitecairns** Abers
29 K4 **Whitecraig** E Loth
2 E4 **Whitecrook** D & G
28 C3 **Whitecross** Falk
74 F4 **Whiteface** Highld
13 L2 **Whitefarland** N Ayrs
15 H7 **Whitefaulds** S Ayrs
58 D1 **Whiteford** Abers
86 d5 **Whitehall** Ork
68 C2 **Whitehills** Abers
58 C3 **Whitehouse** Abers
24 D6 **Whitehouse** Ag & B
30 D3 **Whitekirk** E Loth
66 B4 **Whitemire** Moray
87 c6 **Whiteness** Shet
58 F2 **Whiterashes** Abers
83 L5 **Whiterow** Highld
66 C3 **Whiterow** Moray
3 J6 **Whithorn** D & G
14 D4 **Whiting Bay** N Ayrs
19 G6 **Whitlaw** Border
15 J5 **Whitletts** S Ayrs
31 H7 **Whitsome** Border
83 L5 **Wick** Highld

83 L5 *Wick Airport* Highld
3 J4 **Wigtown** D & G
27 L7 **Wildmanbridge** S Lans
75 K4 **Wilkhaven** Highld
28 F5 **Wilkieston** W Loth
28 C7 **Wilsontown** S Lans
19 G6 **Wilton Dean** Border
28 E4 **Winchburgh** W Loth
64 E5 **Windhill** Highld
68 B3 **Windsole** Abers
38 E7 **Windygates** Fife
83 K5 **Winless** Highld
27 L7 **Wishaw** N Lans
17 J3 **Wiston** S Lans
17 K3 **Wolfclyde** S Lans
38 B2 **Wolfhill** P & K
42 F4 **Woodend** Highld
28 C4 **Woodend** W Loth
68 E6 **Woodhead** Abers
29 H5 **Woodhouselee** Mdloth
10 D6 **Woodhouselees** D & G
59 G2 **Woodland** Abers
6 E3 **Woodland** S Ayrs
58 E6 **Woodlands** Abers
39 G5 **Woodside** Fife
47 K8 **Woodside** P & K
28 D6 **Woolfords** S Lans
38 F3 **Wormit** Fife

Y

18 E4 **Yarrow** Border
18 E4 **Yarrow Feus** Border
18 F4 **Yarrowford** Border
87 d3 **Yell** Shet
86 b5 **Yesnaby** Ork
37 L6 **Yetts o'Muckhart** Clacks
28 B7 **Yieldshields** S Lans
26 F5 **Yoker** C Glas
69 G7 **Ythanbank** Abers
68 C6 **Ythanwells** Abers
69 G7 **Ythsie** Abers

Speed camera locations

Speed camera locations provided in association with RoadPilot Ltd

RoadPilot is the developer of one of the largest and most accurate databases of speed camera locations in the UK and Europe. It has provided the speed camera information in this atlas. RoadPilot is the UK's pioneer and market leader in GPS (Global Positioning System) road safety technologies.

microGo (pictured right) is RoadPilot's latest in-car speed camera location system. It improves road safety by alerting you to the location of accident black spots,

fixed and mobile camera sites. RoadPilot's microGo does not jam police lasers and is therefore completely legal.

RoadPilot's database of fixed camera locations has been compiled with the full co-operation of regional police forces and the Safety Camera Partnerships.

For more information on RoadPilot's GPS road safety products, please visit **www.roadpilot.com** or telephone 0870 240 1701

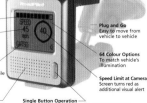

GPS Antenna
microGo is directional, it only alerts you to cameras on your side of the road

Visual Countdown
To camera location

Your Speed
The speed you are travelling when approaching camera

Camera Types Located
Gatso, Specs, Truvelo, TSS/DS5, Traffipax, mobile camera sites, accident black spots, congestion charges, tolls

Voice Warnings
Only if you are exceeding the speed limit at the camera

ALARM MODE

Plug and Go
Easy to move from vehicle to vehicle

64 Colour Options
To match vehicle's illumination

Speed Limit at Camera
Screen turns red as additional visual alert

Single Button Operation
For easy access to speed display, camera warning, rescue me location, trip computer, congestion charge, max speed alarm, date and time